BYGONE BADASS BROADS

52 Forgotten Women
Who Changed The World

ABRAMS IMAGE, NEW YORK

Editor: Samantha Weiner
Designer: Diane Shaw
Production Manager: Rebecca Westall

Library of Congress Control Number: 2017949397

ISBN: 978-1-4197-2925-6
eISBN: 978-1-68335-233-4

Printed and bound in the United States
10 9 8 7 6 5 4 3 2

Abrams Image books are available at special discounts
when purchased in quantity for premiums and promotions
as well as fundraising or educational use. Special editions
can also be created to specification. For details, contact
specialsales@abramsbooks.com or the address below.

ABRAMS The Art of Books
195 Broadway, New York, NY 10007
abramsbooks.com

FOR MOM
My Original Badass Broad

TABLE OF CONTENTS

006 Preface

008 Empress Xi Ling Shi

011 Hatshepsut

014 Agnodice

017 Trưng Trắc & Trưng Nhị

020 Queen Arawelo

023 Fatima Al-Fihri

026 Murasaki Shikibu

029 Khutulun

032 Sayyida Al-Hurra

035 Mochizuki Chiyome

038 Doña Ana Lezama de Urinza & Doña Eustaquia de Sonza

041 Lady Margaret Cavendish

044 King Christina of Sweden

048 Julie d'Aubigny

052 Sybilla Masters

054 Sybil Ludington

057 Anne Lister

060 Ching Shih

063 Mary Anning

066 Mary Seacole

069 Friederike Mandelbaum

073 Lakshmibai, The Rani of Jhansi

076 Stagecoach Mary Fields

079 Isabella Stewart Gardner

082 Emily Warren Roebling

086 Buffalo Calf Road Woman

089 Mary Bowser & Bet Van Lew

093 Marie Duval

096 Fannie Farmer

099 Juliette Gordon Low

102 Annie Jump Cannon

105 Clelia Duel Mosher

108 Sarah Breedlove

111 Edith Garrud

114 Emmy Noether

117 Alice Ball

120 Dorothy Arzner

123 Nwanyeruwa

126 Rukmini Devi Arundale

129 Mariya Oktyabrskaya

132 Irena Sendler

135 Ursula Nordstrom

139 Elvira de la Fuente Chaudoir

142 Jackie Mitchell

145 Noor Inayat Khan

148 Fanny Blankers-Koen

151 Kumander Liwayway

154 Azucena Villaflor

157 Angela Morley

160 Maria Tallchief

163 The Mirabal Sisters

166 Lorraine Hansberry

170 Bibliography

PREFACE

In college, I was a frustrated history major.

Having grown up on American Girl dolls, *Where in Time Is Carmen San Diego?*, and every historical fiction novel about a precocious young woman I could find, when I got to university, I discovered that, if I wanted to continue to study the stories of the women who had made me love history, I wouldn't find them in my survey classes. Women showed up when suffrage was discussed, and there was always cursory attention paid to Queen Elizabeth, Rosa Parks, Hellen Keller—all amazing women, but if I wanted to learn about nonwhite, nonwestern, not straight women, or any women beyond that token handful, I had to take a specialized course, the curriculum of which was usually overwhelmingly about white, straight, cisgender, non-disabled women.

Most people I talk to had the same experience with history classes throughout their schooling. According to these classes, it seemed that women were too busy being oppressed by the confines of their gender to make history.

When I started doing research on my own, I found the complete opposite was true. As long as there has been recorded history, there have been women in the narrative—complex, ambitious, villainous, and virtuous women, who made remarkable contributions to the world long before Rosie the Riveter flexed on the poster. There were so many women who had left a huge impact on the world around them, and yet I had never heard about them in any of my history classes, even through public school and years of university. No one had ever talked about those ladies.

So I started talking about them.

As an author of historical fiction with a small twitter platform of people who generally seem to enjoy weird history as much as I do, I took to social media. Every week, I would tweet about a different woman from history I found fascinating, subversive, and who I had never heard about in my history classes. To my surprise and delight, the series took off, and each week, more and more people would tune in for the next installment of what I lovingly hashtagged #BygoneBadassBroads. The stories began inspiring art, school reports, bedtime stories, new hobbies, and hundreds of people to know their names and to do more research about these women.

And now—joy of joys!—these forgotten stories have been compiled in this book.

Many of the women I chose to highlight over the course of the Twitter series and in this book are morally complex. They are sometimes violent, ruthless, and downright criminal. When their actions are either illegal or unkind, their role as featured women in this book in no way condones the paths they've chosen, but *Bygone Badass Broads* is my attempt to put women back into the historical narrative and to portray them as the complex, three-dimensional humans they were, rather than deny them both a seat at the table and the complexities of personhood we grant men. In order for women to achieve true equality in historical narratives, we have to talk about them in the same way we do men—warts and all.

This book is a collection of the stories of 52 of my favorite women from history. They span time, the globe, socioeconomic situations, sexual and gender identities, and races. They are queens, scientists, athletes, politicians, spies, warriors, peacemakers, criminals, and scoundrels. They are trendsetters, barrier breakers, innovators, and rebels. Each one of them has shown me an infinite number of ways to be a strong woman and a strong human being, and I hope you, dear reader, find in their stories strength and inspiration to be the next generation that changes the world.

EMPRESS XI LING SHI

2700-ISH BCE, CHINA

The Legendary Inventor of Silk

The story of Empress Xi Ling Shi is so wrapped up in legend it's hard to know what's real and what's mythology. But no matter how much of her story is true in the strictest sense of the word, she's an important figure in Chinese history.

Also, "wrapped up" is a really great pun.

Keep reading—you'll get it in a minute.

Xi Ling Shi, also known as Xilingshi, Lei Tsu, or Leizu, was the teenage bride of Emperor Huangdi, the Yellow Emperor, who boasted an impressive resume that included founding the religion of Taoism, creating Chinese writing, and inventing the compass and the pottery wheel. Emperor Huangdi ruled China between 2697 and 2597 BCE, when cloth manufacturing was still a new and confusing process and the silk that put China on the international trade maps had not yet been discovered.

Until Empress Xi Ling Shi.

The story goes that the empress was sitting in her garden, drinking a cup of tea, when a cocooned bug dropped into her cup from the branches of the mulberry tree hanging over her. Defying feminine stereotypes, the Empress did not freak out over the bug—instead, she fished it out of her tea and examined it. The heat of the tea had begun to separate the filament of the cocoon, and Xi Ling Shi began to unravel it.

From that one small cocoon came yards and yards and yards of bright, strong filament, encasing one of the tiny worms that had been making an all-you-can-eat buffet out of the leaves of the mulberry trees in the royal garden.

That was when she had a thought.

Xi Ling Shi approached her Emperor husband and asked him if he would indulge a crazy idea she had: Instead of getting rid of the worms that had been ravaging their mulberry trees, she wanted to plant more trees for these worms to chow down on, then unfurl their little cocoons and make cloth from those fine fibers. Being an innovator himself, the emperor was super on board.

Xi Ling Shi discovered silk filaments, becoming the world's first sericulturist (raw silk manufacturer—don't worry, I also had to look it up) and the inventor of silk looms. She studied silkworms, fed them different foods in experimentation, and discovered that a diet of mulberry leaves produced the best silk. She assembled a squad of women in her court and taught them to weave the cocoons into a super fine, beautiful cloth. The cloth they produced secured a Chinese monopoly that lasted for thousands of years on what the ancient world collectively agreed was the most amazing fabric ever—silk.

Silk became a luxurious, expensive item, widely traded and smuggled along the Silk Road, a trading route that stretched from China to Rome. For two thousand years, only the Chinese knew the secret to its production, making sericulture one of the longest kept industrial secrets in the world.

The discovery of silk and its production were so important to the history of her country that Empress Xi Ling Shi became a Chinese deity, called "Silkworm Mother," or Can Nai Nai. Not a bad way to be remembered.

The story goes that the Chinese monopoly on silk lasted until around 300 CE, when a Chinese princess was afraid she wouldn't be able to get silk in her new homeland of India when she was married to an Indian prince. So she smuggled silkworm cocoons out of China in her hair. The rest, as they say, is history.

The legendary tale of the Empress's discovery was recorded by Chinese academic and philosopher, Confucius.

HATSHEPSUT

C. 1508–1458 BCE, EGYPT

Egypt's First Female Pharaoh

Hatshepsut didn't need a military coup, violent revolution, or backdoor assassination to ascend to the throne of Ancient Egypt, and she didn't need any of those things to hold onto it either. All it took was a little brains, a little talent, and a lot of being in the right place at the right time.

Hatshepsut was born into the ruling family of Egypt but was never slated to be the one in charge. When her father, Pharaoh Thutmose I, died suddenly, Hatshepsut's half-brother/husband Thutmose II (don't think about it too hard—inbreeding was a common way to make sure the crown stayed in the family in Ancient Egypt) took the throne and made Hatshepsut his queen. But Thutmose II died young, and his official heir—Hatshepsut's infant stepson and Thutmose's son by another woman—was too young to govern.

A woman had never ruled Egypt before, but Hatshepsut executed ye old power grab before you could say "nonmilitant takeover," installing herself upon the throne until the baby pharaoh was "old enough" to rule (in quotes, because Hatshepsut had no intention of giving up the pharaoh-ship once she got her hands on it).

She was Egypt's first female pharaoh, and her reign would last for twenty-two brilliant years.

"I HAVE ALWAYS BEEN KING."

As a woman in the ultimate position of power, Hatshepsut had her work cut out for her in establishing the legitimacy of her claim. Image is everything for a politician, so she immediately commissioned multiple statues of herself as Pharaoh, many of which depict her with a beard, at her request, likely as a way of showing that she had just as much authority and right to rule as any man. Then, to stay popular with the people, she undertook an enormous HGTV-style renovation of Egypt, commissioning dozens of ambitious building projects around the Nile. The most impressive was the temple of Hatshepsut at Deir el-Bahri in Thebes, as well as a ten-story obelisk dedicated to her accomplishments and inscribed with the very modest statement, "I have always been king."

Hatshepsut's rule was a time of peace and prosperity, which she used to expand trade routes and diplomacy with Egypt's neighbors. She established a friendly relationship with Punt, a neighboring region on the northeast coast of Africa, and began prosperous trade between the two nations. Trade with Punt included importing valuable goods like myrrh, which you might know as one of Jesus's birthday presents.

After two decades of aggressively successful ruling, Hatshepsut died in what would have been her forties. Her stepson, Thutmose III, the former-baby heir apparent in whose stead she had been ruling, took the throne after her death. He was not as into Hatshepsut's kickass accomplishments as everyone else was and ordered her monuments defaced, statues of her pulled down, and records of her scrubbed from Egyptian history. He took all credit for her accomplishments, and history almost forgot about Hatshepsut entirely. Egyptologists didn't know she existed until 1822, when they were able to decode the hieroglyphics on the walls of Deir el-Bahri, near where she was buried.

In 1903, the British archeologist Howard Carter discovered Hatshepsut's sarcophagus, but it was empty (most of the tombs in the Valley of the Kings, where she was buried, were). After almost a century of searching, her mummy was recovered in 2007. It is now on display in the Egyptian Museum in Cairo.

AGNODICE

THIRD CENTURY CE, GREECE

The Midwife Disguised as a Man

It seems absurd that men could have so much control over a woman's reproductive health, what women could do with their own bodies, and the fates of the babies that they birthed.

Oh, sorry — I'm talking about Ancient Greece, not contemporary America.

I will allow that things have improved since Ancient Greece—for example, most of us no longer subscribe to the once-popular medical belief that women's uteruses can migrate around their bodies and make trouble. And in Ancient Greece, only men were allowed to be physicians—women were banned from the profession for fear that they might perform abortions. The nerve.

So let's talk about Agnodice.

Agnodice was a woman with a mission. From an early age, she knew she wanted to be a doctor, and she knew she wanted to help women. As a teenager, she moved to Alexandria, Egypt, where women were allowed to practice medicine, and she studied until she could deliver a baby with one hand tied behind her back (but she did not do this, because she was a good doctor).

Then she cut her hair and moved back to Greece disguised as a man, determined to save the lives of women as Athens's first female gynecologist. Although no one knew that female part, yet.

Agnodice quickly ran into a problem with her business model: in spite of not being allowed to be doctors, only women were allowed to aid with birthing and midwifery in Ancient Greece. When she would approach a woman in labor and offer to help make sure the birth went well, she'd be thrown out because she was a man. Or rather, she was dressed like one.

"A CERTAIN MAIDEN NAMED AGNODICE DESIRED TO LEARN MEDICINE AND SINCE SHE DESIRED TO LEARN SHE CUT HER HAIR, DONNED THE CLOTHES OF A MAN AND BECAME A STUDENT"

Gaius Julius Hyginus, Fabulae

So Agnodice used the best verification of her gender she could think of: she'd flash the pregnant mother a view of, shall we say, her womanhood. Which usually got her the job.

But the male physicians of Athens were soon onto her, primarily because they noticed all their female patients were abandoning them to seek the care of a scrappy new kid, and they got jealous. Then suspicious. Agnodice's gender was revealed and she was put on trial for her deception. The punishment for her crimes was execution.

Things were looking grim in the courtroom, when a surprise witness showed up. Or rather, a whole fleet of witnesses—all the women Agnodice had treated, ready to raise a militant defense for their lady gynecologist.

Agnodice was acquitted and allowed to continue practicing medicine. No flashing required.

After so many hundreds of years, it is almost impossible to verify whether the story of Agnodice is fact or fiction. Her life comes to us through a combination of oral tradition and a written account by Gaius Julius Hyginus, a Latin author from the first century CE. But either way, it's one of the favorite legends of the medical community. And it's just so badass, how could I not include it?

TRƯNG TRẮC & TRƯNG NHỊ

C. 12–43 CE, VIETNAM

Liberators of Vietnam

Here's an incredibly simplified overview of the political situation of what is today Vietnam. In the early days of the Common Era, Vietnam was under the control of the Chinese Han dynasty. The Chinese had overthrown the Vietnamese government in 111 BCE and annexed the entire country. The Vietnamese people suffered as their culture was stifled, their leaders overthrown, and their lives disrupted by the tyrannical laws of their new foreign overlords.

This is the world into which Trưng Trắc and Trưng Nhị were born, in the province of modern day Mê Linh. They were the daughters of a Vietnamese lord and grew up educated in both books and war.

Neither Trưng Trắc nor her husband, Thi Sách, were into the whole oppressive Chinese rule thing, especially when a new Chinese governor took over their province and started taxing necessities like salt and fishing in the rivers until he had squeezed every last drop out of the insolent Vietnamese peasants.

So Trưng Trắc and Thi Sách started plotting. What if they mobilized the aristocracy? And fought for independence? Against all of China? What if they won? And then reestablished a new, Vietnamese government?

They were dreamers.

But Thi Sách had a bad habit of running his mouth about how aggressively unhappy he was and how great it would be if someone dropkicked the Chinese out of Vietnam.

The Chinese took notice of his vocal opposition and had him executed. His body was hung from the city gates as a warning to other would-be rebels that their Chinese despots were not to be messed with. They assumed that having disposed of the most vocal opposition to their rule, their continual micromanagement of Vietnam was guaranteed.

"Wrong, jerks," said Trắc. "Because I'm still here."

Or something like that.

Trắc picked up where her husband left off. She even had a fearless second in

command, just as she had been to Thi Sách — her sister Nhị. The Trưng sisters began gathering what they probably thought would be a small people's army limited mostly to residents of their village. But their call to arms went viral, and suddenly they had sixty-five cities and eighty thousand soldiers volunteering to take up arms against the Chinese and looking to the Trưng sisters for leadership.

Neither of the sisters had formal military training, but Nhị was a fighter and Trắc was a politician, and they were both freaking fearless. The Trưng sisters chose thirty-six women from their volunteer ranks—including their mother—and trained them to be generals. These ladies then led eighty thousand soldiers against the Chinese, with Trắc and Nhị (who possibly rode elephants—history is a little fuzzy on that one) leading the charge.

And those eighty thousand soldiers kicked the Chinese army out of Vietnam.

After their victory, the people proclaimed Trưng Trắc to be their ruler. They renamed her Trưng Vương or "She-king Trưng." With Nhị still in place as badass number two, Trắc established her royal court in the sisters' hometown of Mê Linh, an ancient political center in the Hong River plain. She immediately threw out all the Sheriff of Nottingham–style taxes imposed by the Chinese and restored a traditional Vietnamese government.

If you're hoping for a happy ending, stop reading here.

After two years of bitching leadership by the people's queens, the Chinese came back like a bad flu, this time with a massive army meant to take Vietnam back from the Trưngs.

But did the Trưng sisters surrender without a fight?

Two words: Hell. No.

For the next three years, the Trưng sisters became warrior tornados of justice, fighting back against China's attempts to reclaim Vietnam.

But they were untrained and outnumbered. As a result, Vietnam fell back into the hands of the Han Dynasty in 43 CE. Surrender was not an option for the Trưng sisters. Neither was dying without their honor still intact. So, with the Han army breathing down their necks, the Trưng sisters committed suicide by drowning themselves.

Their final act of defiance was refusing to die by the hands of the Chinese.

The Trưng sisters have inspired centuries of independence fighters, and today, they are hailed as the first liberators of Vietnam in stories, poems, plays, shrines, temples, monuments, annual celebrations—even postage stamps.

QUEEN ARAWELO

C.15 CE, SOMALIA

The Queen of Gender Equality

This story starts like any fairy tale: Once upon a time, in the land that is present-day Somalia, there was a kingdom ruled by a strong and beautiful queen known throughout her kingdom as Queen Arawelo. She was the firstborn daughter of a brutal king whose hobbies included deflowering maidens, starting wars, and gorging himself on fresh goat marrow. When he died, his only legacy was a trio of daughters—no male heir. Which, if you've ever read a Western fairy tale, is a problem. And if this were anything like a fairy tale, there would be some sort of arbitrary contest with mattresses or a riddle to find the princess a husband to take the throne for her, because patriarchy.

But because this is Arawelo's story, she took the throne for herself.

Because matriarchy.

Her first order of business: tossing stereotypical gender roles from her kingdom.

Before her official rule began, Arawelo was already used to doing work traditionally meant for men. When she was younger, and drought and famine roundhouse-kicked her kingdom, she organized a group of women to fetch water and hunt, the sort of physical labor usually done exclusively by men. When she officially took power, Arawelo was ready to shake things up. Citing the past decades of war that had stricken Somalia as evidence that men break everything they touch, she packed her government with women.

"NEVER HAVE CONFIDENCE IN ANY MAN."

Under Arawelo, girls ran the world, and their men stayed home, took care of the children, and cleaned.

Arawelo's new decrees regarding gender roles and government appointments passed the Furiosa Test—meaning they got men's rights activists riled up. When husbands across the land protested the shake-up, Arawelo and her massive populous of feminist badasses staged a kingdom-wide walkout, leaving their men with nothing but a note on the pillow: Roses are red, gender's performative, your ideas about women are so hella normative. That is not how history actually records it, but they did stage their own Day Without

Women, abandoning their homes for a day to prove just how essential they were.

Since Arawelo lived so long ago, and since she was such an iconic figure, her story, like many others, has become wrapped up in myth. Depending on who's telling it and what they thought of her, you hear many different versions of how the law was laid down in her kingdom. Some say she was a man hater who incited women to seize weapons and get violent. Some say she castrated all the men in her kingdom, which strikes me as questionable just because of how counterintuitive that would be to procreation. Some say she castrated all men except a very select few who she used as breeding stock. Other versions say that, under her rule, rapists were hanged by their testicles (that's the version that I like best).

Whatever the case, Arawelo had cojones of her own to propose and impose such radical notions of female leadership in Somalia. But to the surprise of no one with a brain and a sense of social justice, it worked out awesomely, and under Arawelo, Somalia experienced a long period of prosperity.

Like her life, Arawelo's downfall is similarly shrouded in legend, though the most popular version among historians is that she was killed by her grandson. However she was felled, Arawelo remains one of the greatest rulers in Somali history and one of the OG feminists of world history. A variation on her name is still a Somalian term for a girl or woman who is assertive and independent. Love her or hate her, all versions of her life acknowledge the mark she left on the Somali people.

It's almost like the phrase "yaaaas kweeeen" was invented for her.

FATIMA AL-FIHRI

800 CE – 880 CE, MOROCCO

Bringing Higher Education to the Modern World

Fatima al-Fihri was born in Tunisia in the ninth century, but when she was young her family moved to what is today known as Fez, Morocco. At that time, Fez was one of the most important cities in the east and a center of Islamic faith. It was a religious and cultural hub, a refuge for immigrants from Africa and the Middle East, and an all-around happening place.

Fatima's father was a successful businessman, so she didn't grow up wanting for much. Fatima, her brother, and her sister, Mariam, were educated in subjects like architecture and science, as well as religion. Their whole family was devoutly Muslim.

So things in Fez were great. Fatima grew up. Got married. Lived well. Was highly educated. And was happy.

And then, all at once, things were no longer so great. Fatima's husband, father, and brother all died in quick succession.

It's hard to look on the bright side when the people you love die, but one good thing came from this trio of funerals: the considerable family fortune passed to Fatima and Mariam.

Though likely tempted to splurge on purchases that would bring them comfort, both sisters wanted to use their inheritance to benefit their beloved Islamic community. Huge numbers of Muslim refugees had been flooding the city, and the mosques in Fez couldn't accommodate the sudden swell in numbers.

So the sisters decided they wanted to give the people of Fez—many of whom were immigrants, as they had once been—a space to worship and study. With her half of the inheritance, Mariam built the Andalusian Mosque. And Fatima used her half to establish the University of Al Qaraouyine.

In 859 CE, Fatima financed, founded, and oversaw construction (she loved architecture, so she was also closely involved in every aspect of design and building) of the world's first modern university, meaning degrees were granted in subjects at different levels depending on which classes students took.

Al Qaraouyine became a center of advanced learning in the Mediterranean. Throughout its thousand-year history, Al Qaraouyine educated many distinguished Muslim and non-Muslim thinkers, including Pope Sylvester II, who introduced Arabic numerals and the zero to Europe (thanks for nothing, Sylvester </pun>). Al Qaraouyine also became an epicenter for the study of natural sciences and architecture, which happened to be Fatima's two favorite subjects.

And wait — it gets even better: The University of Al Qaraouyine, founded by Fatima in 859, is still granting degrees to this day.

"THE COLOURS OF THE UNIVERSE ARE THERE BECAUSE OF THE EXISTENCE OF WOMANKIND."

Sir Muhammad Iqbal

Fatima's library at Al Qaraouyine has been restored by another badass lady, Canadian-Moroccan architect Aziza Chaouni, and a wing is now open to the public.

There are a few historians who claim that the story of Fatima founding a university is entirely fake—created by the internet to counteract stereotypes about Muslims and support the "women did it!" propaganda of the modern feminist movement. Unsurprisingly, the majority of proponents of this theory are dudes. A lot of the arguments get into technicalities of wording in historical records from the time, as well as translations from Arabic. I reject this argument out of hand, but I feel obliged, as a person who writes nonfiction, to put it out there.

MURASAKI SHIKIBU

PROBABLY C. 973-1014, JAPAN

The World's First Novelist

We don't know much for certain about Murasaki Shikibu.

We don't know what year she was born, when she died, or what her real name was, and we can't really pin down an exact timeline or date for most of the events in her life.

What we do know is that she was a rule-breaking rebel poet in eleventh-century Japan.

From an early age, Murasaki was defying all conventions of daily life in Heian period Japan. Her mother died when she was young, and Murasaki was raised by a single dad. Convention number one—SMASHED! Women and men in Heian Japan were traditionally raised and lived separately. In her father's household, Murasaki studied Chinese alongside her brothers—another convention, SHATTERED. Chinese, the language of the government, was taught only to men. Growing up, she read Buddhist classics and was trained in music, art, and calligraphy—make sure you don't trip on the pieces, because that's another convention SHATTERED! Murasaki received a

man's education from a father who often lamented that she wasn't a boy, because she was smarter than all her brothers.

It didn't matter to Murasaki that she was born a girl. She was still ready to change the course of literature forever.

And then, as is typical in eleventh century documentation, details about her life get a little fuzzy from here. We know she married a distant relative and had a daughter with him. He died not too long after. We know Murasaki's father received a government position in the province of Echizen, and she followed her family to the imperial court, where she was given a position as lady-in-waiting/writer-in-residence to Akiko (Empress Shōshi), the teenage empress of Emperor Ichijō. The Empress surrounded herself with courtiers who wrote poetry and diaries as they lived in seclusion, celebrating the arts. They welcomed Murasaki into their ranks, and she was able to nourish her passion for prose at the dopest artists' colony in Ancient Japan.

This is around the time Murasaki probably started writing *The Tale of Genji*, a long-form piece of narrative prose considered to be the first modern novel.

"NO ART OR LEARNING IS TO BE PURSUED HALF-HEARTEDLY."

The Tale of Genji, it should be noted, is enormous. With fifty-four episodes and a word count that's twice that of *Moby Dick*, it follows the timeline of four generations, featuring almost four hundred characters. The central character, Hikaru Genji, the Shining One, pursues love and happiness through life in courtly Japan, like any good chosen-one story, until karma bites him in the ass and he's exiled to die in obscurity.

The Tale of Genji was an instant bestseller. Hand-copied editions were distributed through the provinces within a decade (okay, I know, that doesn't seem like an instant bestseller, but remember, it's the 1000s and news travels really slowly). Within the century it was considered a classic of Japanese literature. Every literate person wanted to take a vacation to the capital to read the copies of Genji in person. To this day, artists and calligraphers still copy out and lavishly illustrate the story.

After five or six years (remember—we know basically nothing for sure) working for the empress, Murasaki retired to the Lake Biwa region. When she died (again, who knows exactly when?), she left behind a three-year diary of life at court, 128 poems, and the first modern novel, thereby paving the way for insecure narcissists to quit their day jobs for centuries to come.

The name we know the world's first novelist by today is likely a composite of the first name of one of the heroes of *The Tale of Genji* (Murasaki is the Japanese word for purple) and a title bestowed to her family due to her father's position at court.

KHUTULUN

1260–1306, MONGOLIA

Wrestling Champion of the Ancient World

Back in the days when they were still warring nomads, the Mongols were the ultimate sports fans. They loved athletics and valued physical strength above almost anything else. Wrestling was where it was at—it's still the national sport of Mongolia, and the thirteenth-century Mongols went nuts for it. But the smackdowns of the day that fans went wild for were continents away from modern wrestling matches—anyone could challenge anyone no matter age, weight, or gender. There were bare knuckles, little padding, and almost no rules.

And if you challenged Khutulun at wrestling, you best have prepared to have your dumb ass handed to you.

Khutulun was the great-great-granddaughter of a fellow called Genghis Kahn. You might have heard of him—he was the guy who started the Mongol Empire, which, at its height, was the largest contiguous empire in history, stretching from China to Europe and the Middle East.

Her father was a fellow named Kaidu, ruler of a portion of this kingdom that encompassed present-day Uzbekistan,

Kyrgyzstan, and part of northern China. He was an old-school nomadic firebrand, who raised Khutulun and her fourteen older brothers to be badasses from birth, and Khutulun was the baddest of asses. She spent most of her childhood (and, TBH, her life) besting the boys in competitions of physical and mental strength and cut her teeth (and won both fame and fortune) in the wrestling ring from an early age.

When it came time for her to marry, Khutulun was aggressively unenthusiastic about the idea of tying her life to a dude. She could never love a man the way she loved slamming him into the ground and seeing the defeat in his eyes as he lay flat on his back in the center of the mat.

Which led to her sweeping declaration that she would marry any man who could defeat her in a wrestling match, but anyone who tried and failed owed her one hundred horses.

Shortly thereafter, Khutulun had 10,000 horses and no husband.

Giddyup.

Khutulun's marriage-wrestling made her a celebrity. She was the Nomadic Mongol Bachelorette, but with full contact sports instead of roses. Each suitor that stepped up to face this wall of a Mongolian princess quickly found his legs swept out from under and his butt handed to him, demolished by the woman he wanted to make his bride. After all the good suitors had been soundly trounced, Khutulun issued a general call for challengers—she'd face anyone who thought themselves man enough to face her. But if you lost, the horse tax still applied.

When one particularly swaggery bro bet one thousand horses he'd pin Khutulun, her parents begged her to throw the match because she needed to just settle down with a nice boy already! Khutulun agreed . . . until she heard the bell and looked that smug dude right in his smug dude eyes, at which point animal instinct took over and Khutulun did what she did best: She threw him to the GROUND.

Not only was Khutulun an undefeated wrestler, but she was also a cavalry soldier with nerves of steel and a kick-ass signature combat move: barreling across no man's-land, grabbing an enemy

"SO STRONG AND BRAVE THAT IN ALL HER FATHER'S REALM THERE WAS NO MAN WHO COULD OUTDO HER IN FEATS OF STRENGTH."

Marco Polo from *The Story of Marco Polo*

soldier in a full nelson, yanking him off his horse, dragging him back behind her line of soldiers, and dumping him at her father's feet. This didn't do a lot strategically, but hot damn was it intimidating. It was Khutulun—not one of those fourteen brothers—who was her father's most trusted advisor on political and military strategy when civil war broke out among the Mongol tribes.

Before he died, her father tried to appoint Khutulun as leader. She refused. But if he was handing out titles, she'd take general.

Khutulun became a general in the Mongol army, choke-holding enemies across Asia and continuing her undefeated wrestling career until she died, probably in battle around age forty-five, unpinned by the patriarchy.

A lot of what we know about Khutulun comes from Marco Polo, who was quite a Khutulun fangirl and wrote extensively about her.

Khutulun did eventually marry, when unsavory rumors began to circle about why exactly it was she wasn't taking a husband. History isn't totally sure who she married, but we know he didn't beat her in wrestling. She was undefeated her whole life.

Khutulun is known in history by several names, including Aiyurug and Ay Yaruq, all referring to moonlight.

The actual numbers of Khutulun's horse winnings are a bit vague. Some people say she got ten horses from every man she beat. Some say one hundred. Either way, it's a lot of horses.

SAYYIDA AL-HURRA

1485–1561, MOROCCO

Mediterranean Pirate Queen

Before we start this entry, let me get something off my chest: We don't actually know this woman's real name.

The name history remembers her by, Sayyida al-Hurra, is actually a title that means "noble lady who is free and independent," or "woman sovereign who bows to no superior authority," which I have been trying to get my friends to call me for years. She's also been recorded under the title Hakima Tatwan, which means governor of Tétouan, the Moroccan city that she ruled. And if history can't remember your name, these are not bad things to be called.

But most modern accounts of her life call her Sayyida, and, in spite of knowing that isn't her name but lacking a definitive answer otherwise, that's what I'll be calling her, too.

So. About Sayyida.

Born in 1485 to a Muslim family in Grenada, Sayyida's childhood took a sharp left turn in 1492, which you may remember was the year Columbus sailed the ocean blue. The rhyme they don't teach you in grade school is that in 1492, Spanish monarchs Ferdinand and Isabella conquered the Muslim kingdom of Granada, and their armies murdered and enslaved a hundred thousand Muslims and forced another twenty thousand to flee.

The Spanish were real dicks in 1492.

Sayyida and her family were among those who fled, and they found themselves refugees in present-day Morocco, starting over with nothing. And from that moment on, Sayyida began playing the long-game of plotting revenge on the Spanish bastards who had displaced her family and murdered her people.

But all in good time.

As a young woman, she married another refugee, who also happened to be governor of the city of Tétouan in Morocco, making her the first lady. In spite of a vast age difference between them, the two seemed to have a real mutual respect for each other. Together they fortified the city and built an enormous mosque.

When her husband died, Sayyida seized the moment—and the throne—and declared herself governor of Tétouan (that's how she obtained the title "al-Hurra," which means queen; she was the last Muslim woman in history to use the title).

This is when her quest for vengeance against the Spanish pricks who destroyed her family and her people really starts. And it starts with a piratical fleet.

Sayyida made an alliance with the Barbary pirates, the scourge of many European trade routes and reigning overlords of the Mediterranean Sea. Under Sayyida's leadership, her new pirate BFFs assembled a fleet that prowled European shipping routes and blasted to bits any ship they encountered that made birth in a country that had exiled and murdered Muslims.

Sayyida then took the money from these looted ships and, after giving her pirates their cut, used what was left to make Tétouan even more awesome. The once floundering area, populated by struggling refugees, was built up, and families who had lost everything when they were banished from Spain were repaid.

As you can imagine, Sayyida was a popular ruler among her people.

Sayyida's actual exploits are, unsurprisingly since we don't even know her name, not well documented. There are stories that she captured the Governor of Portugal's wife and hold her for ransom, and others that she personally led onshore raids in Gibraltar. Some accounts say she never actually set foot on a ship, just ran her piratical empire from the throne room of Tétouan. What we do know for sure is that, for twenty years, Sayyida ruled the western Mediterranean with a fleet

"THE UNDISPUTED LEADER OF THE PIRATES IN THE WESTERN MEDITERRANEAN."

The Forgotten Queens of Islam
by Fatima Mernissi

of pirate boys at her beck and call and revenge in her heart.

In 1541, she married the King of Morocco, but despite being a bona fide queen with bigger landholdings at her fingertips, she refused to give up her governorship of Tétouan. Or her piratical extracurriculars.

We're not totally sure what happened to her after that. She was dethroned by her son-in-law in 1542, at which point she disappears from the books all together. There are no records of her death.

But it seems fair to assume that our Muslim pirate queen/actual queen/yas kween slipped from the throne and into the canon of historical badasses the same way she did everything else—like a boss.

MOCHIZUKI CHIYOME

SIXTEENTH CENTURY, JAPAN

The Widow Who Trained Ninjas

Sixteenth-century Japan would have made Westeros look like a children's book. They didn't call it the Warring States (Sengoku) period because it was peaceful. A 175-year conflict was raging. The Japanese Emperor was largely a figurehead overlooking an internal bloodbath playing out between feuding nobility as they fought for power and territory by slashing each other's faces with katanas.

It was a brutal, violent time to be alive, and almost everyone lost someone in the conflict.

Including Mochizuki Chiyome.

When her husband, Moritoki, became a casualty of no one being able to get along in Japan, she was taken in by her husband's uncle, the nobleman Takeda Shingen. Takeda Shingen had promised his nephew that, should Moritoki die in battle, he would take care of his wife.

And ho boy did he ever.

When Chiyome arrived on Takeda Shingen's doorstep, she was already an iron lady trained in martial arts and espionage. She was descended from Mochizuki Izumo-no-Kami, an epic martial arts master, as well as a line of warriors who had once owned a booby-trapped ninja academy disguised as a pharmaceutical company. So, though Shingen likely planned for "taking care of Chiyome" to mean giving her somewhere to sip tea and be a lawn ornament, Chiyome had a different offer for him: What if she helped him with the war he was fighting (and also with the relatives who were trying to assassinate him because of the aforementioned samurai on samurai murder-fest for power)?

Shingen was super on board for that.

With Shingen's blessing and patronage, Chiyome set up a camp in the village of Nezu. She billed her establishment as a religious sanctuary where women could seek refuge from the horrors of war.

But actually, it was a secret training school for lady ninjas.

Chiyome would travel to war-ravaged villages and recruit orphaned moppets, widows, and any other such down-on-their-luck girl who needed a fresh start and was handy with a sword. The rest of Japan saw this and likely mused upon how cute it was and what a nice, charitable, kind, normal woman Chiyome was.

They never suspected that what was really happening in Nezu was basically an action movie training montage in which Chiyome transformed these scrappy little nobody girls into stone-cold badass warrior women.

Known as kunoichi, Chiyome taught her students how to pass themselves off as maids, shrine maidens, traveling entertainers, religious pilgrims, noblewomen, priestesses, and dancers to gain access to their enemies' inner sanctums and gather secrets. The students were drilled in etiquette, dance, singing, disguise, and infiltration techniques to help them blend in with high society. A pretty basic finishing school education until you add martial arts, what to look for in the enemy base, memorization techniques, and how to hold out under torture.

And then she sent them out into the field to fight for Takeda Shingen.

The lady ninjas planted forged documents, passed messages, poisoned water supplies, and spread false rumors. Occasionally they slit a throat or two. Though they never saw combat, they stole secret information, listened in for assassination plots, scoped out city defenses, and were generally critical to the war effort. All under the watchful tutelage of Mochizuki Chiyome.

Between 1561 and 1573, it's estimated she had around three hundred agents throughout Japan feeding information directly back to her so she could pass it to Takeda Shingen.

I wish I could regale you with stories of these women backflipping between pagodas and throwing ninja stars into the enemy's eye, but we don't know many details of their subterfuge because Chiyome didn't want evidence of their exploits on company letterhead, so their missions weren't recorded. Let's just say that turning a convent full of widows and orphans into a steel-edged cadre of warrior saboteurs that infiltrated war-torn Japanese society . . . that's badass.

After Shengen died, Chiyome was never again mentioned in history. She simply disappeared into thin air, along with all her agents.

Bad. Ass.

DOÑA ANA LEZAMA DE URINZA & DOÑA EUSTAQUIA DE SONZA

1600s, PERU

The Vigilante Duo that Cleaned Up Peru's Toughest Town

Before we begin this story, which is so awesome it will melt your face off, allow me to set the scene:

Potosí, Peru, one of the roughest towns in 1600s South America or anywhere maybe of all time ever. Imagine the wealth disparity of Panem in *The Hunger Games* packed into a city the size of London. Half of Potosí was throwing Jay Gatsby–style ragers and drinking champagne from glasses made out of hundred dollar bills, while the other half was eating dirt, dying slowly of horrible diseases, and wearing extra layers in an attempt to protect themselves in case they got stabbed on their way to the grocery store.

But somehow, these two worlds merged when an urchin named Ana Lezama de Urinza met Eustaquia de Sonza, daughter of a thrower of the Jay Gatsby parties in what is tragically unrecorded but probably history's greatest meet cute.

Eustaquia had the sort of life where servants with palm fronds brought her diamond plated martinis, but like many rich girls, she was lonely. Not for a friend—she wanted a hot girl to get it on with (which in history is often coded as "friend"). Which is where Ana, a street rat from the wrong side of the tracks, came in.

But they didn't mention that part to Eustaquia's father when they asked him if Ana could officially be adopted into their solid gold household.

Eustaquia's dad was on board—there would be another girl for his beloved daughter to do stitching and tea drinking and lady things with!

But Ana and Eustaquia could not have been less interested in stitchery.

They wanted to learn to fight.

Ana and Eustaquia shared a passion for sword fighting, and since Eustaquia had indulgent parents, they were soon studying with master fencers. When they became too good for their fencing masters, they decided to take their skills to the streets and deal out vigilante justice to the criminals menacing the innocents of Potosí.

Since it wasn't super appropriate for ladies to be roaming unchaperoned through the lawless Gotham landscape of Potosí, Eustaquia and Ana went in disguise. Each night, they left their villa dressed in dude duds and prowled the streets, looking for skulls to crack. They were the queer, femme Batman and Robin of Peru.

Carousing their way through the streets of South America's rowdiest city, these two muchachas-in-disguise wandered between bars, drinking, dancing, and gambling until they spotted an innocent in danger. Then out came the swords.

In one of their more famous battles, Ana and Eustaquia were up against four banditos. Like any badass action duo, the gals fought back-to-back. When Ana was cracked in the jaw and lost consciousness, Eustaquia went into full-on Rambo mode. She took on ALL FOUR MEN ALONE to protect her wounded girlfriend, and damn if she didn't take those sons of bitches down.

Don't worry—Ana staggered back up to her feet and cut off the hand of the dude who had clocked her.

The now-handless bandito and his dumb buddies all fled.

For five years, Ana and Eustaquia attended the finest parties in ball gowns, then whipped off said ball gowns in a dark alley when the bat signal flashed. They would race to the aid of the citizens of Potosí, doing their part to make the crime-riddled and dangerous streets a little less crime-riddled and dangerous. Eventually it got around that it was actually two women dolling out justice and they became known as the Valiant Ladies of Potosí.

The couple retired when Eustaquia's father died and left the girls his entire estate. But clearly, they still did their fair share of hell raising, because Ana died a few years later after being gored by a bull (tragic, yeah, but what a badass way to go). Eustaquia went into mourning for Ana and died just four months later of a broken heart.

To this day, the Valiant Ladies of Potosí remains one of the most popular folk tales in Peruvian history.

Like many queer woman from history, we can't know for sure if Ana and Eustaquia's relationship was truly a romantic one. But their story bears a lot of the codes we use for queer women in history.

The Valiant Ladies of Potosí have become legendary to a point that it is hard to separate fact from fiction when studying their lives. Primary sources are scarce, and the ones that do exist often lean hard into legend. I've re-created what I can based on the sources I found, but there's a lot of room for storytelling in the re-creation of their lives.

LADY MARGARET CAVENDISH

1623-1673, ENGLAND

The Original Sci-fi Geek

If 1600s England had a Comic Con, the longest signing line in the convention center would have been for Margaret Cavendish, Duchess of Newcastle-upon-Tyne, a woman whose name and title, though lengthy enough on their own, include no mention of the fact that she also wrote the first science-fiction novel.

Like many woman of her age and social station, Margaret had an excessive number of siblings and no formal education. Since it wasn't fashionable for ladies to be book smart, she educated herself in secret. And because of all the excessive siblings, no one noticed.

As a young woman, she lived in exile as a maid of honor to the English Queen in France (this was all during the English Civil War, which was a complex and dangerous time to be associated with certain members of the royal family). When she returned to England, she had a husband and a newfound desire to pursue the study of science, thanks to the salon-style roundtables she'd been part of on the Continent. The problem was that the world of science was a world mostly inaccessible to women of her time. But her husband, who was also an amateur natural philosopher (*scientist* wasn't a word yet), supported her interests and helped her connect with men like Thomas Hobbes, Robert Boyle, and René Descartes, who all contributed to her scientific education.

And apparently, she took to it quite quickly, because in 1663, Margaret published the book *The Philosophical and Physical Opinions*, wherein she put forth some complex theories about atomic movement and their cooperation to form complex organisms (she also snuck in a passionate plea for more educational opportunities for women). The following year, she published another work in which she challenged ideas of many contemporary natural philosophers, all while suffering ridicule for being the first recorded English woman to write with the intent of publication under her own name. At the time, women who wrote weren't expected to want to share their work widely—any writing they undertook should be created only as something fun to pass around among their friends (for reference, two hundred years later, women like the Brontës and George Eliot were still publishing under male pseudonyms in order to be taken seriously).

But she kept writing.

Margaret was a prolific author with an absurd number of published poems, essays, plays, and prose over her lifetime, but let's talk specifically about her novel *The Description of a New World, Called the Blazing World.* You may recognize the basic plotline from any number of modern portal fantasy novels: a lovesick merchant sailor kidnaps a woman, walks through a doorway at the North Pole into a utopian steampunk dream world of WTF where sentient half-man, half-animal creatures make up the population and giant airships crowd the sky. Our main character becomes their Empress and, with her otherworldly subjects, explores natural wonders and does science.

What makes it different from every other portal fantasy is that a compelling case can be made for *The Blazing World* being the first science-fiction novel ever written.

Like any good science-fiction novel, Margaret used her imagined world to ask questions about where science was going in her real world, as well as examine the changing relationships between God and man as Enlightenment sensibilities steamrolled their way through historic theology. She also looked at gender roles (the two main characters are women, and Margaret also uses self-insertion, briefly making herself a character, thereby pioneering the field of the Mary Sue), power, and politics.

The introduction to the book, written by Margaret, began "To All Noble and Worthy Ladies . . . And if (Noble Ladies) you should chance to take pleasure in reading these Fancies, I shall account my self a Happy Creatoress."

So not only did Margaret write one of the earliest science-fiction novels (if not the earliest), she wrote it for the girls.

In her personal life, Margaret was a fashionista. She loved wearing unusual clothes (this lady was made for modern geek culture—she would have been a rad cosplayer). She was bawdy and outspoken in public, believed in animal rights, criticized her society's obsession with constant technological advancement (the world never really changes, y'all). She was extravagant and flirtatious, swore frequently and with great relish, and earned the nickname of Mad Madge among the social elite.

Unfortunately, one of her least good ideas was acting as her own doctor, and as a result of not getting a second opinion, she died in 1673.

Margaret was the first woman to be invited to observe experiments at the new Royal Society of London, a forum for male scientists of the day. Unfortunately, also the last for a while: A ban on women in the Royal Society lasted until 1945. Which is, frankly, an unacceptable length of time.

I would be remiss if I did not footnote another of my favorite historical ladies, Mary Shelley, who was another early science-fiction writer. She's well known enough that I decided not to include her in this book, but a compelling argument can also be made for *Frankenstein* as the first science-fiction novel. Whatever the case, a genre now owned by bros who call women fake fans and lead gamergate was founded by ladies. Think on that.

KING CHRISTINA OF SWEDEN

1626–1689, SWEDEN

The Gender Non-Conforming Nerd Who Ruled Sweden

Everyone was excited when Christina was born.

Because, for a few hot seconds, they all thought she was a boy.

As you've probably guessed from the title of this book, she was not.

While many kings have smashed furniture with rage over the fact that their inaugural child wasn't male, Christina's father, King Gustav II Adolph, was super chill about it.

She might have been a girl, but he wasn't going to raise her like one.

As the royal firstie, the king made sure that, despite her X chromosomes, Christina would receive the sort of education usually reserved for princes.

Christina inherited the crown when Sweden was neck-deep in the Thirty Years' War, a conflict that began with the Holy Roman Emperor restricting religious activity in his kingdom and escalated from there. Her father died in said war when she was nine. Since Christina was too young to rule and Sweden was sensible about not wanting a preteen in charge, a regent was put on the throne until she came of age, and two women were appointed by the court to raise the girl-king. They weren't romantically involved with each other, but basically Christina grew up with two moms.

Under her two moms, Christina became the sort of royal child who, were she the heroine of a young adult novel, would be a cliché: super spunky, a little out of control, a great lover of books (she would study for up to ten hours at a time and spoke eight languages), and so not interested in traditionally feminine things. She was notoriously ungainly (her evil chancellor [more on him later] hired a ballet troupe to teach her to be graceful) and could usually be found looking unkempt, wearing men's clothes, and swearing like a sailor. She was also a crack shot and a lover of filthy jokes and adventure stories.

TL;DR: androgynous girl king who loves learning and pants, coming of age in a war and wanting peace, under the control of a war-mongering regent.

Buckle up, here comes the evil chancellor.

While Christina was busy coming of age, Count Axel Oxenstierna, Chancellor of Sweden, was controlling the country in her stead, and he was the evilest. He loved war—had it been admissible under Swedish law, he would have married war. He was an enthusiastic supporter of Sweden keeping up the good fight in the Thirty Years' War and tried to go around his lady king's back and send a war-advocating delegate to a peace conference.

Luckily, Christina double-crossed his double-cross and sent her own delegate to advocate peace and get Sweden the hell out of the war. Then she kicked out Oxenstierna and put her butt on the throne, where it rightfully belonged.

Now that King Christina had pulled her country out of war, she decided to make it an intellectual capital of Europe.

Under Christina's rule, Stockholm became the Athens of the north. If I listed all the things Christina studied and all the scholars she invited to her court, we'd be here for the rest of the book. From theater to Islam to Greek dance, just to name a few. She was pen pals with Descartes and established one of the best art collections in Europe. She inspired the first Swedish newspaper and the first countrywide school ordinance. Basically, it was nerd central.

Christina was also a badass politician. She'd been active in politics since age fourteen (an age at which most of us were the sort of irresponsible knuckleheads that would have accidently blown up any Scandinavian country we were placed in charge of) and kept the postwar turmoil from turning into internal conflict in Sweden. She was renowned, too, for her militant protection of personal freedoms, for her charities, and as protectress of Jews. She also had her issues. She was a major patron of the arts, which isn't a cheap endeavor, and she ran the country into a bit of debt.

But overall, Christina was a great big nerdy nonbinary lady king.

And she was super not interested in getting married.

At age nine, Christina had read a biography of Queen Elizabeth I and decided that the virgin queen had the right idea with the no men thing. So, she made a sweeping declaration to never marry.

No one took this seriously, because who takes anything a nine-year-old decides about their future at face value? But guess what? She never did marry. Despite how adamant the men of the Swedish court were that the lady king should marry and make babies and have a man king to man rule, Christina refused.

What did Christina have instead of a husband? Well, probably a tattoo that said, "trample the patriarchy" with a little smiley unicorn.

But also, she had ladyloves. Specifically, her lady in waiting, Countess Ebba Sparre. The two women wrote passionate love letters, and Christina called Ebba her "bed fellow and companion." Christina had a man beheaded for calling Ebba a Jezebel and spreading rumors about her two timing, then probably got another tattoo commemorating shutting down slut shaming biphobia.

So, everything seemed to be going great in Christina's court, where "Single Ladies" played on repeat and there were free JSTOR credentials for all.

But then, ten years into her reign, Christina abdicated the throne.

Why? We don't really know. Neither did Europe.

Maybe because she wanted to be a Catholic, which was illegal in Sweden.

Maybe because the pressure to marry became too much.

Whatever the reason, at twenty-seven, Christina stepped down as king of Sweden and fled to Rome, dressed as a man.

"IT IS A FAR GREATER HAPPINESS TO OBEY NO ONE THAN TO RULE THE WHOLE WORLD."

She then proceeded to spend the remainder of her days shocking European society with her wild ways and refusal to be traditionally feminine. She was friends with four popes, and Louis XIV, who thought she was a baller for showing up in his court wearing pants. And at one point she tried to talk herself onto the thrones of Naples and Poland. Which didn't work. But good hustle, Christina.

Christina died in 1689, an intellectual nonconforming nerd rebel to the end. Her tomb is in St. Peter's Basilica in Rome.

Many historians have speculated as to how Christina would have identified had she been alive today and had our modern vocabulary for sexuality and gender identity and what pronouns she would use. There is also some speculation as to whether she was intersex (an exhumation of her body was inconclusive). Since there is literally no way short of time travel for us to know for sure, I chose to use *she*, because assigning historical figures different pronouns than they used or labels that they would not have known existed makes me feel squicky.

A note on Christina's cross-dressing: It was a really big deal at the time for a lady to not wear lady clothes (and, disappointingly, still is in many places). Homosexual relationships between women weren't really taken seriously unless one of those women started acting like a man. The seventeenth century was not on board with gender bending.

JULIE D'AUBIGNY, AKA LA MAUPIN

1673–1707, FRANCE

Bisexual Swordswoman, Opera Singer, Hell-Raiser

Julie d'Aubigny was many things: notorious duelist, seducer of nuns, cross-dresser who left a string of broken hearts and bitter enemies across Europe, and if none of that interests you, I'm not sure why you're reading this book.

Born in 1673 in France, we're not entirely sure Julie is her real name—all we know for sure is her stage name, La Maupin. But she was often credited as Julie in cast lists when she became a singing sensation, and Julie d'Aubigny is the name she is most commonly known by today. Her mom was out of the picture at an early age, and her dad, a vice-riddled rogue who trained royal pages for the French court, seemed to really wish his darling little girl were a darling little boy, because he trained her alongside them in swordsmanship, riding, hunting, and all those other manly man activities of the seventeenth century.

This unorthodox education might explain Julie's early predilection for wearing boys' clothes, waving swords about, and getting to know gentlemen. Often in the biblical sense.

In the tradition of centuries of protective fathers, Julie's dad had a habit of dueling any man ballsy enough to court his daughter. When she realized she'd have to take on some creative problem-solving if she ever wanted to get laid, Julie shacked up with the only dude her father couldn't get away with dueling—his boss.

Which was when her dad decided they should probably get her married.

Julie, however, decided probably no.

When an engagement was arranged between Miss Julie and a milquetoast royal clerk, Julie let everyone know exactly how she felt about it by running away to become a performing fencer.

As a teenage fencing prodigy, Julie traveled France with a rascally swordsman who became both her lover and business partner, performing demonstrations with the sword to crowds that went nuts for this skinny girl who could sling foils with the brawniest of men. Those years of pageboy training had made Julie so good that, during one demonstration, a sexist douchebag in the audience voiced doubt she was really a woman, because ladies can't fight that well.

So, Julie flashed him her boobs.

While dueling.

Which was proof enough.

But Julie had a short attention span when it came to everything, and she soon grew tired of her swordsman lover. Especially when she caught the eye of a local merchant's pretty blonde daughter. Upon discovering their kid was queer as a three-dollar bill, the girl's parents decided the best thing to do was separate her from Julie by getting her to a nunnery.

No problem for Julie—she took the veil, too.

Together they had secret nun liaisons in the House of God. And when they were discovered, they took the body of a newly deceased nun (she died of natural causes—don't worry, Julie is many wicked things, but she's not a nun-murderer), hid it in her bed to cover their escape, and burned their convent down on their way out the door.

And this was all before she turned twenty.

Alas, after three months of blissful post-convent elopement, Julie was bored again and left her girlfriend for a new mistress: the theater. Julie became an opera superstar in France, under the stage name Mademoiselle Maupin. Audiences went wild for Julie both because she had a unique voice (one of the first and only contraltos on stage at the time) and because she had the sort of personal life the 1700s tabloids would have eaten up. Julie's hobbies included singing, gambling, seducing men, seducing women, seducing women while dressed as a man, and dueling men who tried to stop her.

"BEAUTIFUL, VALIANT, GENEROUS AND SUPREMELY UNCHASTE."

Gallant Ladies by Cameron Rogers

In spite of dueling being illegal in France, Julie was notorious for going out of her way to pick fights with anyone who looked at her wrong. When a gentleman in her opera company was being a misogynistic creep toward women backstage, Julie doled out some vigilante justice: She followed him home after a rehearsal, beat him in the street with a cane, and stole his watch. The next day at work, while he was telling everyone the story of how he got jumped by several huge men on his way home, which is where the giant bruises on his face came from, Julie pulled out the stolen watch.

"Surprise, chump," she said, probably.

Her romantic exploits were similarly legendary, as was her fondness for cross-dressing, which carried forward from her youth. It only seemed to be a problem to the men of France when she stole the attention of pretty girls away from them. At a royal ball, Julie (in her male garb) noticed a girl all the men were after, took it as a challenge, and pretty soon the two were making out on the dance floor. All the men who were after this girl were pissed, so Julie suitably dealt with the conflict: by taking them into the courtyard, whipping out her rapier, and whooping all their asses.

She should have been condemned to death for dueling, but the king of France, Louis XIV, thought it was so awesome that he pardoned her.

La Maupin was a drama queen, on stage and off. During a brief stint in Brussels (possibly a banishment due to excessive dueling) she stabbed herself with a real dagger on stage to get the attention of the Elector of Bavaria, her current gentleman caller whose affection had been wandering. Surprisingly, this did nothing to win back his attention and instead scared him off. He offered Julie 40,000 francs to part on good terms, and though one would think the friendzone stinks a little less with a cash bonus attached to it, Julie threw the coins in his face, cussed him out, and pushed him down the stairs.

And then, as mysteriously as she arrived on the historical scene, Julie vanished. We know very little about her later life, only that she died around the age of thirty-seven from unknown causes.

As the poet hath wrote, only the awesome die young.

SYBILLA MASTERS

1676–1720, UNITED STATES

Mother of All (Patented) Inventions

It's hard to say with any certainty whether Sybilla Masters was the first female inventor in America, primarily because most women inventors throughout history had to wade neck-deep through such a swamp of sexism and bureaucracy, with men in charge refusing to recognize their achievements, that many gave up and just let the credit go to someone with a penis.

And Sybilla faced her share of swamp-wading, too. But she persisted.

Sybilla first shows up in colonial American records in 1692, when she testified in a New Jersey court. Before that, we can best speculate that she was born around 1676 in Bermuda and immigrated with her family to New Jersey when she was young. Sometime between 1693 and 1696, she married Thomas Masters, a Quaker merchant, and they moved to Pennsylvania.

It was Thomas's name that had to go on Sybilla's first patent, since women were not legally allowed to have patents issued to them. Most American colonies weren't even issuing patents at the time, including Pennsylvania, so Sybilla had to schlep all the way to England to get King George I to issue a patent to her husband for her process of "Cleaning and Curing the Indian Corn Growing in the several Colonies of America." Sybilla had invented a wooden cylinder and a series of heavy pestles, powered by a horse or a water wheel, which expedited the process of making a corn meal called Tuscarora rice, which was sold as a cure for tuberculosis.

Sybilla might have suffered in anonymity for her discovery, but her husband was a boss. Even though the patent legally had to be issued to him, he made sure it stated it was for "a new invention found out by Sybilla, his wife," and that everyone knew it. So, he's a top-notch feminist in my book.

When Tuscarora rice failed to take off as an export, Sybilla received her second patent for a method of weaving straw and palmetto leaves into hats, bonnets, baskets, matting, and furniture. She also somehow talked her way into a monopoly on palmetto leaves, and as soon as her patent was issued, she opened a hat shop in London where she was essentially printing money thanks to her unique process for weaving.

Until 1793, Sibylla remained the only woman to have patented an invention.

SYBIL LUDINGTON

1761–1839, UNITED STATES

The Patriot Who Mustered a Militia

Listen, my children, and you shall hear
Of the teenage girl who outrode Paul Revere.

Sybil Ludington was born in 1761, the oldest of twelve children belonging to a family who were naught but humble farmers in Duchess County, New York. She came of age during the American Revolution, when colonists were getting sick of British shenanigans and the British were getting tired of their mouthiest overseas investment. When the Revolutionary War broke out in earnest, Sybil's father, Henry Ludington, who had started running with the Sons of Liberty in 1773, took control of the local militia.

A thing to remember about the militiamen who fought in the American Revolution: They were mostly untrained, soldier-ish men with day jobs. Most worked their farms and shops until the alarm sounded, then out came the pitchforks and the patriotism. They weren't super organized, trained, or uniformed, and they were going up against one of the sleekest war machines in the world: the British army.

Colonel Ludington commanded a band of these scrappy young farmers-by-day, hobby-soldier-militiamen-by-night, who lived throughout New York. On April 26, 1777, British soldiers slipped into Danbury, Connecticut, and started burning that sucker to the ground. Danbury flashed the bat signal in the form of a messenger sent to Colonel Ludington's house, who showed up, at night, in the middle of a storm, and delivered the news that Danbury was under siege. The militia needed to be mustered. The problem was that said militia was scattered all over New York.

"Don't worry," said sixteen-year-old Sybil. "I got this."

Though most parents wouldn't trust their teenagers with car keys, Colonel Ludington had shared spy codes and secret signals with Sybil so she could aid the resistance. She was also a fantastic rider with a beloved horse named Star. So, when she volunteered, the colonel didn't hesitate—he sent his daughter out on horseback in the middle of the night to rouse his militia.

The ride was dangerous. Sybil had to navigate treacherous wooded terrain in the dark and the rain and avoid loyalists who would turn her in to the British soldiers. At one point, she had to fight off a highwayman who accosted her. She clocked him with the musket she had slung on her back and pressed forward.

Over the course of the night, Sybil rode more than forty miles, going from town to town, barreling through streets, and shouting at an ungodly decibel to rouse the men from their beds and get them soldiering. At dawn, she returned home, soaked and exhausted, and found that, thanks to her efforts, four hundred militiamen had gathered at her father's house. The militia arrived too late to save Danbury, but by God they gave the Regulars hell on their way out.

"THANKS TO HER DARING, NEARLY THE WHOLE REGIMENT WAS MUSTERED BEFORE HER FATHER'S HOUSE...AND...WAS ON THE MARCH FOR VENGEANCE."

Willis Fletcher Johnson's *Colonel Henry Ludington: A Memoir*

For her efforts, Sybil received personal thanks from two of my favorite Broadway rappers, George Washington and Alexander Hamilton.

Sybil and her beloved Star continued to work as messengers throughout the remainder of the Revolutionary War. She and her sister also guarded their home when there was a bounty on their dad's head. Imagine these badass girls prowling their property with muskets. No one messed.

Postrevolution, Sybil married and had a son. She and her husband were innkeepers, and when he died, she ran the business on her own. Sybil died at the age of seventy-seven, in the nation she helped build. Her legacy lives on in statues sculpted by Anna Hyatt Huntington located in Carmel, New York; Washington, DC; Danbury, Connecticut; and Murrells Inlet, South Carolina. There are also markers along her route and a commemorative stamp upon which she rides like the bat out of hell that she was.

For reference, Paul Revere rode only about twelve miles (and was also a plagiarist, a naval disaster, and an awful silversmith), so I'd like to know where is the poem about Sybil that we have to memorize in elementary school?

ANNE LISTER

1791–1840, ENGLAND

The First Modern Lesbian

Tucked away in the English countryside, amid rigid social structures, landed nobility with their stiff upper lips and equally stiff rules about decorum, at a time when the Bennett sisters were worrying about balls, emerged Anne Lister, often called the first modern lesbian.

Though "emerged" seems like a rather tame word. Burst. Exploded. Smashed her way double-fisted into a world of men, ran their businesses, and stole their wives.

Whatever. Anne Lister arrived.

Anne was born in 1791 to a prominent military family in West Yorkshire. Being a child of a roguish and tomboyish nature in a world where young women were encouraged to be simpering and demure, Anne was sent to boarding school at a young age to throw some water on her spitfire spirit.

And then promptly thrown out of boarding school because she was getting busy with her roommate, the first in a long line of ladyloves for Miss Lister.

During her time at boarding school, and over the course of her life, Anne kept extensive diaries, most written in a code she invented, which was a combination of Greek, punctuation, and algebra. Why employ this code? Because she was writing openly (and often explicitly) about her life as an astonishingly self-aware queer woman in the 1800s. Over the course of her life, Anne wrote four million words worth of diaries, the code of which wasn't broken until the 1930s. They are now considered the Rosetta Stone of nineteenth-century lesbianism, or, as writer Emma Donoghue put it, "the Dead Sea Scrolls of lesbian history," one of the most modern and frank accounts in existence of being a queer woman in the pre-twentieth-century Western world.

With her education completed through a combination of boarding school and home correspondence courses, adult Anne proceeded to become the Lady Casanova of West Yorkshire, seducing damsels from Harrogate to Halifax and making little secret of it. As both a devotee of her library and a woman in a time when homosexuality was at best frowned upon, Anne developed a rather sly version of nineteenth-century gaydar. She'd figure out if a woman was interested in a bit of a snog behind the schoolhouse by mentioning books with queer themes and seeing how prospective girlfriends reacted.

Imagine, if you will, a young Anne sidling up to lovely lady at a party, batting her eyelashes, and simpering from behind her fan, "Oh I just love that divine scene in the *Achilleid* when Achilles dresses as a woman and dances for Patroclus . . . don't you?"

Books are sexy.

Anne often dressed in men's clothing while out on the town, and was called Gentleman Jack by both her ladyloves and the scandalized townspeople of West Yorkshire. Like any good regency rake, she had a long string of tumultuous affairs, both domestically and on the Continent, but Anne was looking for something a little more committed. She wanted a partner. She came close with the great love of her life, Marianne Belcombe, but their romance ended in separation and heartbreak when Marianne married (okay actually five years after that, but it's fine, her husband was cool with it). But before you despair that this is yet another tragic lesbian story that ends in forever alone, Anne found love again with wealthy heiress Ann Walker.

And in 1834, reader, Anne married her.

Married being a loose term, as there wasn't any legal foundation for the union of two women in Georgian England. But Anne and Ann found a chapel and some rings and a rogue religious man willing to bind these two in holy matrimony despite their gender, which is good enough for me.

Anne was not just a queer woman in a time when "sodomy" was a capital offense. She was also a savvy businesswoman at a time when there were precious few ladies doing business. In her twenties, she became the owner and manager of her beloved family estate, Shibden Hall. She managed tenants, renovated the house (this included adding a library tower and a secret passage, because priorities), turned a profit from her farmland, and developed a colliery (if you, like me, need to Google this term, let me help—it's a coal mine). She then took the money she was rolling in as a result of her lit estate and used it to invest in railways, canals, properties, mines, and quarries.

Aside from her life of business and lesbianism, Anne loved to travel, and she developed a passion for mountaineering. In 1830, she became the first woman to ascend Mont Perdu in the Pyrenees.

She died of a fever at the age of forty-nine, while abroad with her wife.

Same-sex relationships were viewed very differently in the early 1800s, and the concept of sexuality was non-existent. This was the time of the romantic friendship, a passionate and often physical friendship between two members of the same gender, and erotic relationships between women were often not taken seriously. They were even encouraged premarriage, and many of Anne's ladyloves were taken to bed with their husband's permission, including her great love Marianne Belcombe. The line was drawn when a women started acting like a man and took on a man's role.

After her death, Anne's diaries went into the attic and remained there until the early twentieth century, when a relative found them and began to crack the code. The content was, shall we say, shocking, so he stuffed them into the Shibden archive. They were finally decoded and published in their entirety by Helena Whitbread in 1988, and can be read, compiled, in *I Know My Own Heart: The Diaries of Anne Lister*.

CHING SHIH

1775–1844, CHINA

Terror of the South China Seas

Like any great legend, the origins of Ching Shih, who was statistically the most successful pirate in history, are shrouded in mystery. She was likely born in Guangdong, a coastal province in southeast China, around 1775, and worked in a brothel as a young woman. She makes her first appearance in recorded history in 1801, when the notorious pirate captain Cheng I took her as his wife. The story goes she only agreed to marry him after he signed a piratical prenup, which entitled her to half his plunder and a hand in all his nautical affairs.

Several years later, when Cheng I got sucked into a tsunami and spat back out in pieces, he left behind a substantial fleet and a bloody reputation. So, his widow, Ching Shih, decided the only sensible thing to do was be even better at piracy than he was.

Ching took over her husband's fleet, made a red flag their symbol, and unified the captains that had gone astray with the following rallying cry: "Under the leadership of a man you have all chosen to flee. We shall see how you prove yourselves under the hand of a woman."

It was pretty effective.

All those captains who had been half-assing their fleet-leader duties came running back to her.

Ching's first order of business was to issue a pirate code to ensure that any wishy-washy dipshits who weren't keen on sailing under the command of a woman either behaved or bailed. The men who sailed under the Red Flag adhered to her strict rules, including:

Rule 1: If any of her men raped a female captive, you better believe that dude was beheaded posthaste.

Rule 2: Sex of any variety gets you thrown in the ocean. Because Ching knew that sexual frustration built up over weeks bobbing upon the vast expanse of empty ocean makes men great at ragey plundering.

Rule 3: Steal from the crew coffer? Ching would chop off your head and fling your lifeless body into the unforgiving sea.

Rule 4: Desert your post? Ears cut off.

Rule 5: Act before the captain gives orders? Bid a hasty farewell to your head.

Ching Shih was not kidding around with her pirate code. Savvy?

With her fleet united under her code and her flag, dyed red with the blood of any insubordinate subordinates, Ching and her men worked their way up the Chinese coast, pillaging, plundering, and being a general scourge to any ships stupid enough to get within the range of their guns. Within a few years, Ching had tripled the size of her husband's original fleet and even managed to unite a bunch of her husband's former enemies beneath her banner. Then she ruled them all.

"UNDER THE LEADERSHIP OF A MAN YOU HAVE ALL CHOSEN TO FLEE. WE SHALL SEE HOW YOU PROVE YOURSELVES UNDER THE HAND OF A WOMAN."

At the height of her piratical reign, Ching Shih was known as The Terror of the South China Sea. She commanded eighty thousand sailors aboard almost two thousand ships, statistics that soundly kick hellions like Blackbeard and Francis Drake in the balls.

For obvious reasons, most notably piratical terror, the Chinese emperor was not keen on Ching and her Red Flag Fleet, as they were called. So, he launched a campaign to take her down.

It did not go well . . . for the emperor.

Instead of running from the navy, Ching faced them head on and blasted their broadsides to splinters. She captured sixty-three ships and convinced most of the emperor's sailors to join her. Her piratical wrath was so legendarily terrible that the Admiral of the Chinese army committed suicide rather than be captured by her.

The Portuguese navy also tried to get her. Failed.

The British navy made an attempt. Failed. Hardcore failed.

Ching Shih was nigh uncatchable.

After years of trying, the Chinese navy finally got tired of having their asses handed to them and offered Ching amnesty. She dropped her anchor and retired like a boss—she spent the rest of her days running a brothel/casino in the Chinese countryside and probably lounging around on piles of treasure.

During the Golden Age of Piracy, the eastern corsairs didn't have the same stigma attached to women being on board a ship as the west did, or the superstition that women on board was bad luck for the ship. Ching Shih was one of many women who sailed, though she's one of the best documented cases of how active these women were in piratical affairs.

MARY ANNING

1799–1847, ENGLAND

The Fossil Collector Who Changed Paleontology

Mary Anning's life began with a lightning strike.

A family friend was holding baby Mary when a thunderstorm began brewing. Before shelter could be sought, the woman was struck by lightning and killed. But tiny indestructible Mary survived, the first of many near-death adventures that would populate her childhood.

Mary grew up in a town called Lyme Regis in southern England, famous for fossils that could be harvested from the surrounding cliffs. After landslides, Mary and her nine siblings would gather fossils from this treacherous landscape to sell to tourists. A totally normal, death-defying chore to have your kid do.

Turns out, Mary was rather fantastic at fossil collection and identification.

When she was twelve, she and her brother found something awesome—the first complete Ichthyosaur skeleton correctly identified.

Mary sold the Ichthyosaur skeleton to a collector and it ended up in the London Museum of Natural History. Remember—she's twelve. The discovery challenged the way people looked at the history of the earth, because back then everyone was into the Bible and not dinosaurs. Mary's discovery was also a key piece of evidence in the argument for extinction, which was a new concept back then.

Did I mention that she was twelve?

The discovery of the Ichthyosaur skeleton made Mary famous, launched her career as an internationally known fossil hunter, and kicked off a longtime love of dinosaurs. In her twenties, Mary found another complete skeleton, this time of a Plesiosaur. It was, again, the first of its kind to be found.

The scientific community lost its mind.

But the men who wrote and published a paper on the discovery of the Plesiosaur never gave Mary any credit for discovering or preparing the skeleton.

Mary found three more Plesiosaur skeletons, and this happened every. Damn.

Time. No credit given to the lady who did all the legwork.

Mary was a self-taught expert in fossils. She was good at finding and harvesting them from the dangerous cliffs around Lyme Regis and could identify the era a fossil came from by sight. Her main collaborator was her best friend, artist and fellow fossil collector Elizabeth Philpot. They were Lyme Regis's dinosaur girl gang. At the age of twenty-seven, she opened her own fossil store and bought a house for herself.

Mary's fossil collecting made her a bit of an international celebrity. People came to Lyme Regis from around the world to buy her fossils. Scientists visited her for research help. The King of Saxony even visited Dorset because he wanted to meet her.

But because sexism is a bitch, Mary was not credited for most of her finds, not admitted to any scientific societies, and published nothing. Her only printed work was a letter to the editor in the *Annals and Magazine of Natural History*, calling them out on getting their facts wrong.

Despite the sexism she endured, Mary was one of the first women to receive an honorary membership to the Geological Society of London. She was recognized by many scientists as an expert in fossils and was often sought out for advice on anatomy and classification.

"THE CARPENTER'S DAUGHTER HAS WON A NAME FOR HERSELF, AND DESERVED TO WIN IT"

Charles Dickens on Mary Anning

Mary died from breast cancer in 1847. After her death, Charles Dickens wrote of Mary Anning, "'The carpenter's daughter has won a name for herself, and has deserved to win it."

But her legacy is truly immortalized in perhaps the highest honor a human being can receive: The tongue twister "she sells seashells by the seashore" was written about her.

Her fossils can still be seen in museums around the world.

MARY SEACOLE

1805–1881, CRIMEA

The Jamaican Nurse on the Crimean Battlefield

It's possible everything you know about the Crimean War can be summed up in two words: Florence Nightingale.

Don't feel bad, she's all that most people know about the Crimean War. Until recently, it's all I knew. And Florence Nightingale was a badass boss lady of history and medicine for sure.

But at the time, her reputation for medical miracles and ministrations was rivaled by a biracial, fifty-something, self-funding, hotel-owning battlefield angel named Mary Seacole.

Mary was born in Kingston, Jamaica, in 1805, the daughter of a Scottish soldier and a Jamaican mother. Because she was mixed race, she was able to avoid enslavement but was still denied many of the basic human rights that white people had, like the right to vote, hold public office, and work certain jobs.

After a short-lived marriage left her a widow, Mary decided that more than another husband, what she wanted was a passport full of stamps. She traveled all over the Caribbean, to Cuba and Haiti and

the Bahamas, as well as to Central America (she made bank for a few years running a store in Panama that sold supplies to men passing through on their way to find gold in the western United States) before setting a northerly course for England. On the way, she got European medical training, which supplemented the traditional Caribbean medicine her mother had taught her. By the time the Crimean War broke out in 1853, she was a full-fledged doctor and had already kicked cholera's ass while working as a nurse in Jamaica.

England was reporting a lack of supplies at the frontlines, a breakdown of nursing care for soldiers in the Crimean War, and that things were generally just not going great. And Mary wanted to do something about it. But when she offered her services to England as a battlefield nurse, they turned her down. She had no hospital experience, had technically never filled out an application, and was past the typical age for nurses. The fact that she was black might have also been a factor, but no one said that out loud.

Thankfully, she had an iron resolve to do good and some cash to spare. Not only did she pay her own way to Crimea, but once she got there, she set up a British Hotel that served as "a mess-table and comfortable quarters for sick and convalescent officers," in an area she dubbed Spring Hill (present-day Ukraine).

At first, it wasn't really a hotel—it was barely a building. It was more of a hut. But between treating the sick and whipping up grub for the soldiers, Mary gathered abandoned metal and wood to build up her hotel.

Once opened, Mary had her fingers in every one of her establishment's pies—both metaphorical pies and literal ones. She cooked. She administered to the wounded. She ordered supplies and sold or sometimes gave them away to soldiers. She visited the battlefield, often under fire, to nurse the wounded and became known as Mother Seacole. She fought prejudice from army doctors who called her a quack because her medicinal training was Caribbean and because she was a woman. Her reputation rivaled Florence Nightingale's, who was known as "the Lady with the Lamp." Mary Seacole was called "the Creole with the Tea Mug."

She assisted the wounded at the military hospitals and was a familiar figure at the transfer points for casualties from the front. Her remedies for cholera and dysentery were particularly valued.

"I HAVE WITNESSED HER DEVOTION AND HER COURAGE . . . AND I TRUST THAT ENGLAND WILL NEVER FORGET ONE WHO HAS NURSED HER SICK, WHO SOUGHT OUT HER WOUNDED TO AID AND SUCCOR [SIC] THEM AND WHO PERFORMED THE LAST OFFICES FOR SOME OF HER ILLUSTRIOUS DEAD."

William Howard Russell

At the war's end she returned to England and declared bankruptcy, having spent every penny she had on doing unto others on the frontlines of Crimea. Her friends, including Queen Victoria, helped her raise money to publish her autobiography, *Wonderful Adventures of Mrs. Seacole in Many Lands*, which became a bestseller and put Mary on top again. It was one of the first travel memoirs published by a black woman.

Mary died of a stroke in 1881.

In 2004, Mary Seacole was voted the Greatest Black Briton. Certainly also a contender for the same title without the racial modifier.

The Crimean War at a glance: Between 1853 and 1856, Russia, Sardinia, Britain, France, and Ottoman Turkey fought in the Crimean Peninsula for a lot of reasons, but in short, Russia was shoving their way into Turkey and everyone was unhappy about it. And also, because, of course, religion was involved.

There is some speculation and accounts from the time that Mary and Florence haaaaated each other. But according to both of them, their styles were different but their relationship cordial. And I'd rather not perpetuate the girl-on-girl hate narrative. So if they say they were cool, I believe they were cool.

FRIEDERIKE "MARM" MANDELBAUM

1818–1894, UNITED STATES

New York's Queen of Thieves

New York City's Queen of Thieves was born Friederike Weisne to Jewish parents in Germany in 1818-ish.

That's about all we know about her early life.

Moving on.

Friederike married Wolfe Mandelbaum and together they immigrated to the United States in 1850, because there are no cats in America and the streets are paved with cheese. The Mandelbaums started their life in New York City as business people—they bought a dry goods store to sell normal goods that were dry.

But you know what's a lot more profitable than dry goods selling?

Crime.

Crime, as it turns out, pays.

After street peddling got her connected with the rascals and rogues that ran the Dickensian dystopia that was the streets of Gilded Age New York, Friederike decided to use her dry goods store as a front for a fencing operation.

Not fencing like swords or the thing Tom Sawyer avoids painting.

Fencing as in buying stolen goods off of criminals and then reselling them at a huge profit.

Her husband, in spite of being in possession of the incredibly badass name Wolfe, was basically soggy cornflakes molded into human form. An acquaintance described him as "weak-willed [and] lazy," so he was totally cool to do the nineteenth-century equivalent of drinking beer and watching football while Friederike built her felonious empire.

Being a criminal overlord takes several essential things: brains, guts, and, most importantly, connections. And not just to thieves, swindlers, and all variety of vile villainy who will keep your store stocked with pinched possessions. You also need a

network of corrupt lawmen on your side. And, knowing the power of the almighty dollar, Friederike paid off scads of New York City politicians, police, and judges, which allowed her to do as she pleased.

By 1864, Friederike's criminal enterprise was so successful that she was going to need a bigger boat. She bought a building on Clinton and Rivington Streets, set up a "haberdashery" shop on the first floor, and built extravagant housing for herself and Wolfe on the top two. For decades, that haberdashery masqueraded as a respectable front for the biggest fencing operation in United States history, where Friederike bought and resold stolen goods, from jewelry and furniture to a herd of goats.

"THE NUCLEUS AND CENTER OF THE WHOLE ORGANIZATION OF CRIME IN NEW YORK CITY."

Friederike was content for a while, until she wasn't. But you can only see *Hamilton* from the front row so many times before you want to start turning that money into more money. So Friederike began investing, in thieves, burglars, and all manner of rapscallions.

With some well-placed bucks and some well-connected henchmen, Friederike became a financer and planner in some of the biggest thefts in New York's history, including the Manhattan Savings Bank Robbery, which resulted in the theft of what today amounts to about $75 million bucks.

Friederike was a lady you wanted on your side. Whenever a member of her gang got in a pinch, she was there with the bail, lawyers, and/or bribes necessary to spring them. Marm once organized a jailbreak to get her favorite piano player out of prison because she missed his sick beats at her wild ragers. Her rampant ring of rapscallions called her "Marm," and she called them her "Little Chicks."

"They call me Marm because I give them money and horses and diamonds," she said, which are the essentials I, too, expect from my mother.

When not fencing, financing heists, and liberating criminals from jail, Marm was known for the fabulously exclusive dinner parties she threw. "Party At Marm's!" became one of the most coveted invites in the city, where the country's most celebrated criminals mingled with New York City's fashionable elite.

But in spite of her fantastic success as Queen of the Thieves, Marm didn't love getting her hands dirty. After all, she was a businesswoman at her heart. And wouldn't it be nice to have a gaggle of pint-sized criminals trained to do your dirty work and then have them owe you their undying allegiance as a result of providing for them?

So Marm founded Mandlebaum's School for Gifted Youngsters, an institute known for polishing up street moppets and turning them into master criminals. While no transcripts were ever transferred to an accredited university, the young ne'er-do-wells she plucked off the street and enrolled began by mastering pickpocketing and petty theft. If you passed those classes, you could declare your major and graduate in scamming, safe-cracking, or blackmail, with a minor in burglary.

Marm's Grand Street School (as it was known) became the most successful training center for aspiring crooks in the city. Among the fledgling felons that Marm nurtured, she was partial to helping women, so they wouldn't "wast[e] life being a housekeeper." Criminal might not be a booth one typically finds at career day, but it beat the backbreaking work in hellish mills many girls were confined to because of their gender and socioeconomic station.

Marm's Hogwarts for Scoundrels closed in 1876 after a policeman's kid snuck in to nark, but her enterprises continued to flourish. She eventually had so much stolen merchandise to sell, she had to buy two warehouses to hold it all.

But, as Marm would attest, nothing gold can stay, and in 1884, the Pinkerton Detective agency brought down the crashing fist of justice on her criminal reign. They sold her marked bolts of stolen silk, and then when she resold them, they shouted "AHA!," whipped off their fake mustaches, and grabbed her.

Don't worry—when they came with the actual warrant, Marm punched one of the detectives in the face.

As they should have anticipated, no mere prison could hold the likes of Marm Mandlebaum. She jumped bail with more than $1 million in stolen diamonds and settled in Ontario. Marm lived out the rest of her life comfortably in Canada, turning up her middle finger at the long arm of the American law from a distance, and died in 1894.

In perhaps the greatest tribute to the Queen of Thieves, several mourners reported having their pockets picked at Marm's funeral.

RIP, Madame.

Marm's protégé from her Grand Street School, Sophie Lyons, aka the Princess of Thieves, could have her own entry in this book. Under Marm's tutelage, she became one of the most successful conmen in New York City at the time. Her signature move was luring men to a hotel room, getting them naked, then stealing their clothes and extorting them for their cash. When caught, Sophie talked her way out of arrest by claiming that the real Sophie Lyons would be too smart to have been caught. And it worked. She eventually retired from criminal life and became involved in the rehabilitation of juvenile delinquents. Her autobiography, which scathingly disavowed Marm's tutelage, was called *Why Crime Does Not Pay*.

LAKSHMIBAI, THE RANI OF JHANSI

1828–1858, INDIA

The Mom Who Fought Colonialism

The story of Lakshmibai, the Rani of Jhansi, begins as a cross between *Cinderella* and *The Bachelor*.

At the age of either seven or thirteen (there is a bit of debate over her birth year), Lakshmibai was a contestant on what was basically the nineteenth-century Indian equivalent of a reality show about finding love. When the Maharaja of Jhansi (an Indian state), Gangadhar Rao Newalkar, sought a wife among all the prettiest girls in his kingdom, Lakshmibai got the final rose, married Maharaja Gandaghar Rao, and became Rani (a Hindu title for queen) of Jhansi. They had a child and a generally happy marriage.

Until (there's always an until) . . .

Their child died in infancy, and Rao became sick. Like most kings, he was skittish about the prospect of dying heirless, so he picked a random child to adopt and called him the next ruler of Jhansi.

Then he kicked it. Leaving his queen and adopted son to rule.

But (there's always a but) . . .

The aggressively colonialist British East India Company, reigning dipshits of India at the time, refused to recognize this adopted son as a legit heir. And with no legitimate ruler, Jhansi was annexed, their military and the royal court disbanded, corrupt British officials installed, and Hindu rituals banned.

(The EIC sucked.)

Lakshmibai, constant champion for her people, decided to take the British to court over her son's right to rule.

But diplomacy got her nowhere because the East India Company, colonialist asscravats, were writing the rules, then rewriting them as needed to royally screw over India.

So, when diplomacy failed, Lakshmibai chose a different tactic: aggressive negotiations.

Twenty-something Lakshmibai declared open revolt, attacked the British fort at Jhansi, recaptured her city, and massacred

the British invaders. Sources aren't totally clear on her direct involvement in the massacre, but it's universally agreed that this is where she transitions from queen mother into full-on Boss Bitch Rebel Queen hellbent on kicking the British out of India by their colonialist asses.

Lakshmibai did a lot of stage crew work for the Indian revolution. She built cannons and a mint and created a supportive political infrastructure. She trained women in fighting, horseback riding (and elephantback riding), and shooting. From her trainees, Lakshmibai assembled a personal bodyguard of iron-jawed women courtiers who needed only a nod from her to turn into rampaging human wood chippers. Women who didn't fight repaired the city walls in secret, under her direction.

Lakshmibai herself fought to prevent the invasion of Jhansi from both rival regional lords and the aforementioned British dingbats. And by fought, I mean she rode into battle with her kid strapped to her back, a sword in each hand, and her horse's reins between her teeth.

Which is just so hardcore, I can't.

But Lakshmibai was also a great ruler, with a heart full of compassion for the downtrodden. She exempted the poor from taxes and sold her jewelry to pay her soldiers and give them more food.

All while rocking the single-mom-to-her-adopted-son beat.

The British were beginning to panic because they hadn't expected India to fight back. They launched a full-scale invasion of Jhansi, bringing a few thousand men and cannons to the border with a plan to blow the state off the map.

Despite staring down the barrel of the world's most powerful empire, Lakshmibai and her army held out for two weeks against the British onslaught, long enough for twenty thousand soldiers to arrive from a nearby rebel province and attack the flank of the British Army.

But don't get too excited, because the rebel army sucked. They were led by dummies that immediately lost all the ground Lakshmibai had won.

Lakshmibai was forced to abandon Jhansi, but she left it the same way she fought for it—on horseback, with her son strapped to her back.

Lakshmibai continued to attack from afar as the British ravaged her beloved Jhansi and died in battle a few months later. Her last requests were that her belongings be sold to pay her soldiers and that her son be cared for.

Today, Lakshmibai is an icon of India's First War of Independence, usually depicted riding into battle with her son strapped to her back. Because seriously, why would you ever want to portray her any other way?

STAGECOACH MARY FIELDS

1832–1914, UNITED STATES

The Steel-Nerved, Gun-Totting Scoundrel with a Heart of Gold

The nineteenth-century American West wasn't the "Go west, young man," big skies, open prairies, men were men, ten-gallon hats sort of mythos we're all familiar with. It was a lawless, postapocalyptic wasteland that would have brought Fury Road to its knees.

There were no rules and no mercy.

It would take a badass, behemoth, ten-ton truck of a woman to survive it.

Like Mary Fields.

Mary Fields was born in Tennessee. She was a slave until her thirties, because American history is the worst. We lose track of Mary until she showed up postemancipation in Cascade, Montana, with a double barreled pistol, a heart of gold, and an iron resolve to raise hell.

Naturally, spitfire Mary went to work for nuns.

The Ursuline nuns of St. Peter's Mission in Cascade needed someone to do the heavy lifting for them around their frontier facility. And Mary, at six feet tall and pushing two hundred pounds, was the perfect candidate

for this so-called men's work. Mary hauled freight and supplies, chopped wood, did stone work and carpentry, dug certain necessary holes, and did supply runs for the sisters over the lawless, unforgiving frontier.

Good thing Mary was a concentrated ball of equal parts "don't mess with me" and "I'll mess you up," compacted so tightly that no fear could get in. She fought off wolves, bandits, and bears to get the nuns their grub.

When Mary wasn't cracking feral wolves in the skull with the butt of her revolver, she could be found building schools for Blackfoot Indian girls. Or—on the entirely opposite end of the spectrum—at the saloon. Nonprostitute women weren't allowed in saloons, but Mary had finagled special permission from the mayor to be served at any bar, any time. Despite being nun-employed, Mary loved booze and cigars and was usually seen with a pistol strapped under her apron and a jug of whiskey by her side.

Mary was not to be messed with. She once bashed in a guy's head for calling her a racial slur. The local paper cited Mary as having "broken more noses than any other person in Montana," and nobody ever debated the claim. When a handyman at the nunnery went around town being all angsty and emo about how a black woman made more money than him, Mary whipped out her six-shooter, challenged him to a duel, and shot him in the ass.

Literally.

Since the Bible has some rather specific things to say about violence of that nature, the Ursuline Sisters sent Mary packing.

But Mary was undaunted. She moved on to her next career: restaurateur!

It was short-lived.

Both the restaurants she opened failed because she was giving out too many free meals to people who needed them.

So, on to career number three—in 1895, Mary applied for a job with the United States Postal Service as a mail carrier throughout the Montana Territory. She was sixty at the time and still freaking rocked the job interview, which involved hitching six horses to a stagecoach. She smoked the other applicants (all dudes half her age) and became the second woman, and the first black person, to work for the U.S. Post Office.

For the next six years, Mary braved blizzards, heat waves, driving rain, and screaming winds to get the mail through. If the snow got too high, Mary would tie off the horses and walk through waist-deep snow to deliver mail to the middle of ass-nowhere Montana. In spite of the lawless wasteland that was her office, Mary and her stagecoach (and also by some accounts a pet eagle) never missed a day of work, never failed to deliver a letter, and were never late once.

Mary left the mail business in 1901 and spent her retirement running a laundry service and dealing out justice with her bulldozer fists to anyone who dared cross her (the story goes that, at seventy-two, she flattened the nose of a man who hadn't paid his two-dollar bill, then told him not to worry about it because the joy she'd gotten out of knocking him on his backside was far more than she would have gotten from his two bucks). She also spent time babysitting and going to baseball games, because a girl's gotta have hobbies. She gave flowers from her garden to the home team and profanity-laced tongue-lashings to the umpires when they called against her boys.

Despite her gruff exterior, the town of Cascade adored Mary. When her house burned down, the whole town rallied to build her a new one in a scene that was undoubtedly straight out of *Little House on the Prairie*. The mayor even wanted to mark Mary's birthday with a townwide holiday, until they realized they didn't know when her birthday was. Mary didn't know either, so she told them a different day every year. Usually twice a year, just to give everyone a day off. No one argued.

Mary died at age eighty-two. Not from wolf attacks or subzero mail deliveries. But liver failure.

It was the whiskey that got her.

ISABELLA STEWART GARDNER

1840 – 1924, UNITED STATES

Patron Saint of the Arts

In the middle of Boston, there is a Venetian palace packed floor-to-ceiling with an eccentric array of art and artifacts that haven't been moved in one hundred years. It was built and collected by a tiny, redheaded hurricane of a woman named Isabella Stewart Gardner, the scandalous queen of nineteenth-century Boston society and patroness of the arts.

Isabella Stewart was born in 1840 to an affluent New York City family. After a good Victorian finishing-school education in Paris, she met and married a Boston old-money gentleman named John (or, as his friends called him, Jack) Lowell Gardener.

In 1865, Isabella and Jack's two-year-old son died and Isabella suffered from intense depression. And since this was back in the day when *travel* was a legitimate treatment for inexplicable mental health ailments, her doctor suggested Jack take his wife to the Continent to cure her of her melancholia.

So Isabella and Jack went on a long, extravagant, rich-person-style tour of Europe.

There, Isabella fell in love.

With Europe, travel, and art.

While in Europe, Isabella started buying stuff. There's really no other word for it besides *stuff*. Art, artifacts, furniture, tapestries, statues, jewelry, pottery—ALL THE THINGS! After that first sojourn across Europe, the couple would travel abroad nearly a dozen times, going to Russia, Turkey, the Middle East, as well as across America. Isabella's favorite destination was Venice. Everywhere they went, she bought stuff and more stuff. Books and papers, art, evangelical items, Rembrandts, Botticellis, Raphaels, instruments, artifacts, Chinese and Egyptian antiquities. Really the only thing the items purchased on her international shopping sprees had in common was that Isabella liked them.

When Jack died, Isabella decided to take the considerable wealth left to her by her husband and build a house in the Fenway area of Boston. But Isabella was not just any lady, so it was not just any house. She designed and oversaw construction of a museum, in the style of a Venetian palace, to house her vast art collection where the public could enjoy it.

Isabella was obsessively involved in the building of her museum. She laid out her extensive collection piece by piece. She

picked out the wallpaper and the stonework. When the painters weren't doing the stucco quite right, Isabella got up on the scaffolding and showed them how she wanted it done.

In all things, Isabella was a boss lady who did what she wanted. She smoked cigarettes. The newspaper claimed she took zoo lions for a stroll in the park. She shocked Boston Society by showing up to the symphony wearing a headband that said, "Oh, you Red Sox." She invited the Harvard Football team over after they beat Yale. Isabella loved football and hosted boxing matches at her home. While the men fought, she danced. The press was horrified and fascinated by her, and Isabella reveled in her scandalous reputation. Her motto was "Don't spoil a good story by telling the truth."

Isabella was not just a collector of art—she also collected men (in a totally nonsexual way). Everyone wanted to be in her circle. She was a gatekeeper of high society, the axel of society in turn-of-the-century America. She knew everyone—artists, poets, politicians, painters, basically anyone who was anyone or might someday be someone—and kept a close inner circle of artistic men around her, including John Singer Sargent, James McNeill Whistler, and Henry James. Though people liked to talk, these relationships were purely intellectual as far as we know—though Isabella did burn all her letters before she died. The archives of her museum hold more than seven thousand letters from one thousand correspondents as testaments to her social-butterfly nature. Henry James, a member of her famous harem of dudes, said that Isabella "is not a woman, she is a locomotive—with a Pullman car attached."

Isabella's museum became a community space for artists, musicians, and Boston citizens of all stripes to enjoy art from around the world, at a time when those things were not as accessible as they are today. In the 1800s, art was mostly for the viewing pleasure of the wealthy—she used her money to make it available to all.

When Isabella died, she left her money to a slew of charitable institutions, including a trust she set aside to keep the museum open. The only condition? Nothing in her museum could be moved around or changed from how Isabella laid it out. The museum is still open—you can visit the lovingly laid out collection in her Venetian palace in Boston.

And if your name is Isabella, you always get in free.

When you walk through the museum, the final painting hanging in the Gothic room is an almost-life-size portrait of Isabella, painted by her friend John Singer Sargent in the style of his fabulously scandalous painting Madame X, which basically broke the art world when it was unveiled. Isabella immediately asked Sargent to give her the same treatment as Madame X. The finished work sent Boston society to their fainting couches. Jack was so mortified he asked his wife never to display it. She agreed, waited until he was dead, then displayed it prominently in her museum.

A lot of the men in Isabella's notorious harem were gay. Isabella was an early champion of gay rights, and she made her museum and home a safe space for her friends and their partners.

The Isabella Stewart Gardner Museum was the site of the largest unsolved art heist in American history. Since Isabella stipulated in her will that nothing could be changed, the empty frames of the thirteen stolen paintings still hang on the wall where the pictures used to be.

EMILY WARREN ROEBLING

1843–1903, UNITED STATES

Chief Engineer of the Brooklyn Bridge

If I was the sort of person who read plaques, I would have learned about Emily Warren Roebling a lot earlier, and my life would have been exponentially more awesome much sooner. But it took me numerous crossings of the Brooklyn Bridge before I noticed the brass plate affixed to each tower, commemorating the lady whose top-notch brain and bitching work ethic is the reason it stands today.

In case you, too, are a person who doesn't read plaques, let me tell you about her.

Emily Warren was born in 1843 to a well-off American family in Cold Springs, New York, the second youngest of a batch of twelve children. Her parents died when she was a teenager, and the family's affairs fell to her oldest brother, Gouverneur K. Warren. And you're not supposed to pick a favorite sibling, but he was Emily's favorite.

In 1864, Gouverneur took his visiting little sister to a military ball, where, from across the room, she made eyes at a handsome soldier just as the music began to swell. His name was Washington Roebling, and in 1865 they were married and collapsed into domestic bliss.

If your definition of domestic bliss involves double-teaming feats of engineering previously unseen in the modern world.

Washington's father, John Roebling, was a bridge engineer, and Washington was following in the family trade of getting people across the water. And once that ring was on her finger, Emily gleefully made that family her family and that trade her trade. When Washington went to Europe to study the use of caissons in building bridges, Emily went, too, and learned at his side. Most romantic honeymoon of all time—don't you love it when two nerds fall in love?

Washington and Emily returned to the United States to find that Papa Roebling was neck deep in the project that he was certain would define not only his career but also modern engineering: He was overseeing construction of a bridge over the East River, connecting Manhattan to Brooklyn.

Spoiler: This will become the Brooklyn Bridge.

John appointed his son Washington as assistant head engineer on the project. And naturally, Washington asked Emily to be his assistant-to-the-assistant head engineer.

They were all set to make history.

But three days into the project, John's toes were crushed by a ferry, and shortly after, he died from complications, because historical medicine is a cruel, ignorant mistress.

So assistant engineer Washington became head engineer of the Brooklyn Bridge, probably after falling to his knees and saying, "I will finish what you started," in a Kylo Ren voice.

Except, while installing the largest pneumatic caissons ever created (which allowed his workers to install the foundation of the bridge underwater), he and the majority of his crew were struck with the feller of many a scuba diver—decompression sickness, or "the bends." Many members of the crew died. Washington survived, but he was blind, partially paralyzed, and bedridden.

With one of the most ambitious engineering projects in history on the brink of collapsing and New York City running panicked circles around itself trying to come up with another engineer with the specialized knowledge to complete the project, Emily stepped up.

"Don't worry," she said. "I got this."

Which is how Emily Roebling became the chief engineer on the construction of the Brooklyn Bridge.

If we're being honest, Emily didn't have the resume for the job. She had no formal engineering training, but she had studied caissons with her husband, visited her beloved brother, taken some correspondence classes at Georgetown University, and was ready to learn on the job about bridge strength, stress analysis, cable construction, and catenary curves, until she had assembled a vast mental library of engineering knowledge.

> ## "IF THE END OF THE WORLD COMES AND CHAOS SMASH OUR PLANET TO BITS, AND WHAT REMAINS WILL BE THIS BRIDGE, REARING ABOVE THE DUST OF DESTRUCTION."
> **Vladimir Mayakovsky's *Brooklyn Bridge*, translation by George Reavey**

Emily became the person in charge on site, overseeing and problem solving day-to-day construction on the bridge. She and Washington worked together to make decisions for the project (as much as Washington could from his precarious repose on the jaws of death), though Emily often had to work alone when Washington was catatonic.

When rumors started to get around about Washington being a nonfunctioning invalid incapable of doing any chief engineering, and that his wife was the real brains of the operation, a petition was raised for him to be replaced. Emily leapt to his defense before the boys club that was the American Society of Civil Engineers. She was the first woman to ever address the group, and she made a fearless, impassioned case for keeping her husband on the project (and herself, but she put less emphasis on that). Thanks to her argument, Washington was allowed to continue leading the project.

And by Washington, I mean Washington and Emily.

Emily worked on the Brooklyn Bridge for fourteen years, doing everything from directing on-site and writing correspondence for her husband to representing the project at political meetings. Washington survived the bends, though he battled the after effects of the illness and treatment for the rest of his life. He later said, "I thought I would succumb, but I had a strong tower to lean upon, my wife, a woman of infinite tact and wisest counsel." Historical OTP, seriously.

On opening day of the Brooklyn Bridge—May 24, 1883—Emily was honored in a speech by Representative Abram Stevens Hewitt, who said that the bridge was "an everlasting monument to the sacrificing devotion of a woman and of her capacity for that higher education from which she has been too long disbarred." She was also the first person to cross the newly completed eighth wonder of the world, in a carriage, carrying a rooster for luck.

She was followed by President Chester A. Arthur.

At this point, most people would say, "I oversaw construction on the bridge project that changed history, I think I can retire now."

Not Emily Roebling.

She went on to receive a law degree from New York University and became one of the first female lawyers in New York at the age of fifty-six. She died in 1903 and is memorialized on unfairly small plaques on the Brooklyn Bridge.

But at least they put her name first.

"Mackenzi," you ask. "What is a caisson?" I am not a science person, but I can tell you that they enable you to build underwater by creating air pressure that keeps the water out, and that's about all I know.

BUFFALO CALF ROAD WOMAN

C. 1844–1879, UNITED STATES

Hero of the Battle of Little Big Horn

Buffalo Calf Road Woman, or Muts i mi u na, grew up in one of the suckiest times to be an American Indian. Though really, once white people came on the scene, there has never been a not-sucky time to be an American Indian.

Buffalo Calf Road Woman was caught in the currents of Manifest Destiny from her youth. Her tribe, the Cheyenne, had been bullied into agreeing to the supremacy of the United States in a treaty signed in 1825, and argonauts were plowing through Cheyenne land on their way to gold rush California, leaving a trail of disease. By the time Buffalo Calf Road Woman was a teenager, half her people had died due to the recklessness of white people.

In spite of agreements with the United States government, the white people planting their flags all over the west could not have cared less about Cheyenne claims. When gold was discovered on Cheyenne land in Colorado, the United States government made an oh-so-generous offer to the Cheyenne: Step away from the gold, and, in return, you can have life on a reservation with less than one-tenth of your land holdings. And then they smiled and pretended like it was an awesome and super fair deal for everyone.

Buffalo Calf Road Woman, like most of the Cheyenne, was not on board with this.

The Cheyenne were among the last free First Nations tribes. Across the country, American Indians were being massacred by settlers. The Transcontinental Railroad was disrupting buffalo migration patterns and making food scarce. The Cheyenne who had gone onto the reservation found the government DNGAF about them. In general, the government DNGAF about American Indians.

These are the conditions that set the stage for the rise of Crazy Horse, a Lakota Sioux who united the Sioux and the Cheyenne to fight against the United States. Buffalo Calf Road Woman, her brother, Comes in Sight, and her husband, Black Coyote, joined Crazy Horse's army.

At the first skirmish between Crazy Horse's army and the United States army, the American Indians were defeated and thus began to retreat. But while everyone else was running away, Buffalo Calf Road

Woman rode into the line of fire to save her wounded brother. The battle is still known among the Cheyenne as the Battle Where the Girl Saved Her Brother, in honor of Buffalo Calf Road Woman.

Eight days later, Crazy Horse and his army met with Custer at the Battle of Little Bighorn, or Custer's Last Stand, which you probably remember in passing from tenth- grade U.S. History class. American soldiers faced down an army of American Indian warriors almost twice their size. The battle is most famous for being, as you might have guessed from the name, the sight of Custer's death. What you probably don't know is that it was Buffalo Calf Road Woman who is credited with knocking Custer off his horse, which made said death possible.

For her bravery in battle, Buffalo Calf Road Woman earned a new name, Brave Woman.

Her ending is rather tragic. Her family was banished from the Cheyenne after her husband killed another man in an argument. They were picked up by the United States army and her husband was executed. Shortly after, Buffalo Calf Road Woman died of either diphtheria or malaria.

Fearing retribution if their versions of Custer's Last Stand were told—the version where they weren't the villains—the Northern Cheyenne tribal leaders called for a ban of silence about the truth of what happened at Little Bighorn lasting 100 summers, which was broken in 2005, when Buffalo Calf Road Woman's story was finally told publicly.

Now let's make sure it stays there.

MARY BOWSER & BET VAN LEW

1800s, UNITED STATES

The Civil War Spy Team

The call was coming from inside the Confederate White House.

During the American Civil War, Jefferson Davis was being brought down from inside his own presidential palace, by a spy duo consisting of two best friends, Mary Bowser and Bet Van Lew.

Mary was born in 1846-ish (maybe?), a black slave on a Virginia plantation owned by the Van Lew family. But as soon as Mr. Van Lew kicked it, his son and daughter immediately freed all the family's slaves, because they knew what they were about and had their heads on straight.

Mary and the Lady Van Lew, named Elizabeth but known affectionately as Bet, became BFFs. In spite of something like a thirty-year age gap between them, they stayed in touch when Mary went north to get an education and then took a gap year to be a missionary in Liberia.

When Mary finished school, she was missing her bestie, Bet, something fierce.

So instead of staying in the free North, she went back to the plantation where she had been raised and where Bet now ruled as lady of the house. Technically Mary wasn't allowed to return to Richmond as a free black woman educated in the North, so she had to pose as Bet's slave to return to her.

Which ended up being helpful when the pair teamed up to burn the Confederacy to the ground.

But I'm getting ahead of myself.

When Mary arrived in Richmond, the Civil War was in full swing and Bet had a new hobby: kicking Confederates between the legs from within the walls of their own capital city. Bet had never been shy about hollering her abolitionist ways through the streets of Richmond, so she was already a bit of a pariah with her friends and neighbors. She leaned hard into that. Bet became a pretend recluse and did a lot of shambling and muttering to herself, so that the city started calling her "Crazy Bet."

Who pays attention to a crazy lady? No one.

Which gave Bet the perfect opportunity to become a badass behind-enemy-lines Union spy master.

Bet coordinated agents all over Richmond and into the South, and helped relay information back to contacts in the North. She went to the Libby Prison in Richmond with food and medicine for prisoners—oh, and also occasionally tools to assist Union soldiers in making their escapes. She even built a secret room in her family house to hide them and sympathizers after said escapes.

Bet was a stone. cold. badass.

And when Mary came home, Bet got a new idea of someone who would make a perfect Union spy.

Spoiler alert: It was Mary.

Because you know who nobody noticed in the 1860s Confederate South? Black women.

Bet got Mary a job as a servant for Confederate president Jefferson Davis's wife, Varina. And from the moment she crossed the threshold of the Confederate White House, Mary began her tireless work of taking them down.

Posing as Ellen Bond, a slow-thinking, illiterate slave, Mary got a job as a servant for President Davis's wife, Varina. Mary had a photographic memory and was able to recite back whole conversations she had

heard only in passing. And because Davis thought she was illiterate, she was able to read, memorize, and then pass back to the Union documents left around his house.

Mary and Bet had secret methods for communicating with each other that would have made James Bond take a knee. Mary sewed messages to Bet on the inside of Varnia's dresses, then sent them out to get altered—the seamstress was also in on their schemes and would pass the dresses on to Bet so that she could unpick the messages. Mary poked holes in the letters of books to spell out secret messages. She coded invoices for supplies to be delivered to the house. Mary hung certain colors of washing on the clothesline to send messages to Bet.

And this drove Jefferson Davis bananas: He knew there was a leak in his house, but he had no idea who it was.

In 1865, near the end of the war, another spy was arrested in the Confederate White House. Mary knew if she was caught too, she'd be executed. It was time to get out of Richmond.

But first, Mary burned the Confederate White House to the ground.

Or rather, she tried. It didn't work. On her way out the door, she set a fire in the basement that was quickly put out, but good hustle, Mary.

Post-War history loses track of Mary. We know she founded a school for black children in Georgia. She traveled and lectured.

She married. In 1995, she was honored for her efforts in spying as an inductee in the U.S. Army Military Intelligence Corps Hall of Fame.

Bet Van Lew was the first in the city to fly the American flag. She stayed there for the rest of her life, though she was ostracized for her Union support, and became the post master general.

Bet Van Lew was inducted into the Military Intelligence Hall of Fame in 1993. Mary joined her in 1995.

"YOU HAVE SENT ME THE MOST VALUABLE INFORMATION RECEIVED FROM RICHMOND DURING THE WAR."

Ulysses S. Grant

MARIE DUVAL

1847–1890, ENGLAND

The Artist Behind Victorian England's Most Popular Cartoon

Before *Dennis the Menace*, Charlie Brown, or *The Family Circus*, there was Ally Sloper, a ruddy-cheeked, working-class man whose attempts to stay one step ahead of his creditors resulted in weekly hijinks that had the working class in hysterics. He was created and illustrated by a man named Charles H. Ross.

Except he wasn't.

Ally Sloper's escapades were actually illustrated by Charles's wife, Marie Duval, continuing the long artistic tradition of men taking credit for the work of women.

Marie Duval was born in Paris and christened Isabelle Émilie de Tessier, though when she began her stage career in London she took on the name Marie Duval, which was less intimidating for English audiences to see on a program (she later called herself Noir, and then S.A. the Princess Hesse Schwartzbourg, so this lady knew her way around a pseudonym). On the unlicensed stages and in the seedy music halls of Camden, she made a name for herself playing men, not uncommon for female actresses of the time. Her most famous role, the titular scoundrel and escape artist of *Jack Sheppard*, was also her undoing—during

a tour of the show, she broke her leg, thus ending her stage career.

Around this time, she married a fellow called Charles H. Ross, the editor of a popular serial magazine called *Judy*. Since she was looking for a new profession, Charles hired Marie as an illustrator for weekly comic fashion sketches.

Marie was living in the glory days of penny dreadfuls and sensationalized serials, which were cheap, disposable forms of entertainment that catered to the lower classes. In spite of having an overwhelmingly female readership, there were virtually no women writing or illustrating for them. Or at least, not under their own names.

Before Charles and Marie's marriage-slash-partnership began, Charles had developed the character Ally Sloper for *Judy*. Ally was the antihero everyman with a tulip-bulb nose and a steadfast determination to earn as much money as he could by doing as little work as possible. However, he appeared only briefly before falling victim to a growing preference for long-form pieces in serials over his standalone escapades. But Ally Sloper reappeared in 1869 with a

makeover that would have impressed Tyra Banks. He had a new design, new theatrics, and a whole new set of jokes.

Because he was now being illustrated by Marie.

"SHE OCCUPIES A UNIQUE POSITION AS THE FIRST LADY COMIC ARTIST, SHOWING THE WAY TO MANY WHOSE TALENTS LIE IN THIS DIRECTION."

F.H. "Women's Work: Its Value and Possibilities." The Girl's Own Paper

Marie had no formal art training, but at the tip of her pencil, Ally Sloper's world expanded. She introduced new side characters and settings and used her background in the theater to create physical humor in her art long before Lucy was pulling the football out from under Charlie Brown—these commonplace comic conventions of the twentieth century were revolutionary in the late 1800s. Even the idea of a reoccurring character was new. Ally Sloper was the first comic strip superstar—by the 1870s, he was *Judy's* most popular character, and Marie was illustrating all his escapades. He became so popular that, in the 1880s, you could buy a whole slew of Ally Sloper merch, including snuffboxes and doorstops for the true Victorian fangirl. He starred in stage plays and later silent films, even influencing Charlie Chaplin's tramp character.

Because we all know the rule that anything that's popular can't actually be that good, most of the serials, comics, and magazines of Victorian England's lower classes, including much of Marie's work, were lost. Even with modern historians on the case, there are still pieces of her work that have yet to be located, and many artists in the comic industry today don't know Marie Duval.

But even if they don't know her name, they owe her a lot.

FANNIE FARMER

1857–1915, UNITED STATES

The Chef Who Leveled Her Measurements

Imagine a world where chefs on the Food Network gave convoluted measurements for recipes like "then you add a lump of butter," and already impossible Pinterest tutorials were made even more maddening by instructions like "add enough yeast to make the bread rise." If it weren't for Fannie Farmer, we might still be suffering in the dystopian horror show of nonstandardized cooking measurements.

Fannie was born in 1857 in Boston, Massachusetts. The Farmers weren't a wealthy family, but they believed in education for their daughter, and Fannie had hopes of attending college, until a stroke at the age of sixteen flayed those plans. Fannie was paralyzed and bedridden for months, followed by years of mobility issues and a lifelong limp. Doctors gently suggested that, for her own sake, she abandon any hope of higher education.

Fannie couldn't do much to contribute to the family livelihood, but she did what she could to keep the house in order. She took up cooking and housekeeping, first for her parents and later for a neighboring family. Turns out she had a real knack for making delicious food, because, when she was back in good physical condition at age thirty-one and able to start an independent life, Fannie enrolled in the Boston Cooking School, the rare sort of academy at the time that took a scientific approach to cooking. In addition to recipes and techniques, they taught nutrition, sanitation, chemical analysis, and finances. Fannie was a star student, and after graduation, she stayed on first as faculty and then, two years later, she was appointed principal.

During her time as principal, Fannie decided she wanted to write a cookbook. She began compiling recipes in what would come to be known as the *Boston Cooking-School Cook Book*. Her publisher, Little, Brown, was not convinced it would sell. They reluctantly agreed to a limited print run, if Fannie would cover the production costs out of her own pocket.

But Fannie knew she was awesome and her book was awesome, and she gambled on herself.

The book sold more than four million copies and saw twenty-one editions during Fannie's lifetime alone.

Her cookbook was unlike anything else available on the shelves of 1800s bookstores, because Fannie's approach to cooking was entirely unique. Her book included notes about food science and the chemical reactions that occur in the food while you mix it. She emphasized nutrition and was an early proponent of the idea that food and health are intertwined (imagine that). She also helped to standardize the system of measurements used in cooking in the United States. Before Fannie, American recipes gave the same sort of cooking instructions I often get from my mom over the phone, and you'd find actual printed instructions like "add a teacup of milk," which is helpful not at all. Fannie's use of actual measurements in her writing, as well as emphasis on leveling them, led to her being called "the mother of level measurements." Her cookbook was the first to use standardized measurements.

Fannie left the Boston Cooking School in 1902 and founded Miss Farmer's School of Cookery. She continued to study nutrition, eventually focusing her work on creating recipes for the sick and convalescent, including thirty pages of diabetic-friendly recipes in her follow-up cookbook.

"IT IS MY WISH THAT IT MAY NOT ONLY BE LOOKED UPON AS A COMPILATION OF TRIED AND TESTED RECIPES, BUT THAT IT . . . WILL LEAD TO DEEPER THOUGHT AND BROADER STUDY OF WHAT TO EAT."

During the later years of her life, Fannie used a wheelchair due to increased mobility issues as a result of her stroke, but she continued to lecture all over the country, including prestigious speaking gigs at Harvard Medical School. Her last lecture was delivered ten days before her death, in 1915, at the age of fifty-seven.

One hundred years later, her cookbook, now known as *The Fannie Farmer Cookbook*, is still in print.

JULIETTE GORDON LOW

1860–1927, UNITED STATES

Founder of the Girl Scouts

Lord Robert Baden-Powell had a problem.

He had founded an organization called the Boy Scouts, which, from the name alone, you might have gathered was rather exclusionary of half the children of the world. All he wanted was to take young men into the woods and teach them how to make tents out of tarps and weave macramé from their struggling facial hair, but the problem was that girls were clamoring to join in, too. Young ladies were showing up at Boy Scout rallies in homemade uniforms and trying to sign up with fake names, and B-P knew something had to be done about it.

Luckily he was seated next to Juliette Gordon Low at a party. She was a fifty-something recent widow from Savannah, Georgia, and she was looking for a purpose in life and some girls to empower.

Called Daisy by her family and friends (and since she was a friend to all girls, I'm going to call her Daisy, too), she was born in the Confederate States during the American Civil War, but the family moved to Chicago when she was young. Daisy was a bright, curious, and accident-prone child whose youth was plagued by everything from the

totally legit-sounding Victorian ailment brain fever, to two fingers broken so severely they almost had to be amputated and an ear infection that resulted in partial deafness. On her wedding day, she got a grain of rice lodged in her ear during the grain throwing part.

Their marriage was a fraught one—her husband was a drinker and a cheater. She spent most of their relationship splitting her time between his home country of England, where she had to bite her tongue and pretend to be happy, and her hometown of Georgia, where she would collapse on the shoulders of her friends under the stress of her failing marriage. As she wafted through upper-crust parties and tried to find fulfillment in charity work (which her husband was against, because he was a major jerk), it became clear to Daisy that she couldn't stay married to this guy. The couple had just started discussing divorce when he died suddenly, leaving Daisy childless and alone in her fifties.

She had no idea what to do with her life.

This is when she met B-P, heard about his problem of plucky young girls looking for someone to teach them skills and confidence, and found her purpose.

Daisy threw herself immediately and enthusiastically into empowering the young women of America, turning them into glorious female warriors, queens of all that they survey. In 1912, shortly after that fateful networking opportunity with B-P, eighteen girls gathered in Daisy's cousin's schoolhouse in Savannah, and the Girl Scouts was born.

"I'VE GOT SOMETHING FOR THE GIRLS OF SAVANNAH, AND ALL OF AMERICA, AND ALL THE WORLD, AND WE'RE GOING TO START IT TONIGHT!"

From the start, Daisy wanted the Girl Scouts to be inclusive. No girl, no matter her race, background, or financial situation, would be turned away. The programs encouraged girls to be independent, active, socially conscious, and to make choices—Daisy herself was a big advocate of letting the girls design their own programs instead of assigning

them. Whenever there was a question about what to do next, Daisy always said, "Ask the girls." It was the girls themselves who decided they wanted to be called "Scouts" in America instead of "Guides" like their British equivalents, a name that became official in 1913. The early Girl Scouts knew Daisy as their goofy, compassionate leader who stood on her head at meetings and told ghost stories on camping trips.

Daisy often used her own money to keep the Girl Scouts afloat, even selling her jewelry when funding was tight. She used her talents for fundraising and public relations, combined with her vast network of friends and supporters.

Daisy died of breast cancer in 1927. Two hundred Girl Scouts attended her funeral, and she was buried in her uniform. One hundred years later, the Girl Scouts are 2.6 million strong—1.8 million girls and 800,000 adults—building courage, confidence, and making the world a better place for all girls, thanks to Juliette Gordon Low.

Hear her womanly roar.

The chief rival of the Girl Scouts was not, as you might think, the Boy Scouts but the Camp Fire Girls, a similar girl group, though they were less into female empowerment and more into reinforcing gender norms. James West, a chief executive of the Boy Scouts, did not approve of many of the activities the Girl Scouts participated in, and when Daisy asked him to merge his group with hers, he refused and went on to try to raise hell for Daisy and her Girl Scouts in every way possible, from harassing Daisy over the name Girl Scouts—he said all the Boy Scouts would quit because they felt it trivialized the word "scout" (which did not happen, FYI)—to trying to block her patent on the trefoil knot badge. Thank goodness Daisy was undeterred by male nonsense.

ANNIE JUMP CANNON

1863–1941, UNITED STATES

Census Taker of the Sky

Annie Jump Cannon was raised with her eyes on the sky.

From the time she was but a small person growing up in Delaware, her mother taught her the names of the constellations, which riveted tiny Annie. As a slightly older person, this love of all things interstellar sent Annie to Wellesley, the women's college in Massachusetts known for turning out a steady stream of badass patriarchy smashers. There, she studied physics and astronomy and a bunch of stuff I am too much of a creative type to understand and graduated valedictorian of her class. Her mentor at Wellesley was a woman named Sarah Frances Whiting, one of the few women physicists in the United States at the time, and I'm obsessed with this cycle of women teaching women science. Especially since it was happening in the 1800s.

While attending Wellesley, Annie contracted scarlet fever, feller of many a *Little House on the Prairie* character. She survived, but the disease left her mostly deaf.

Did this stop her? Hell no. Slow her down? Don't be absurd.

She used it to her advantage.

The relative silence, she'd later say, allowed her to concentrate more fully on her work.

Through a lot of fortunate connections, Annie was able to enroll as a special student of astronomy at Radcliffe College, which was Harvard for girls, because heaven forbid we let ladies in classrooms—an impressionable lad's mind might wander from his studies upon seeing the outline of the female form.

At Radcliffe, Annie met Edward Charles Pickering, a BFD in astronomy and physics at the time. He saw in Annie a potential BFD. He hired Annie to join his all-women team of "computers" in the Harvard Physics Department, who were working on mapping and defining every star in the sky and developing a system for classifying them. While the men at the lab operated the telescopes and took photographs (two tasks, it should be noted, that Annie was also more than capable of doing), the computers examined the data, carried out astronomical calculations, and cataloged those photographs. Annie and the other women worked six days a week for twenty-five cents an hour.

Annie and her fellow computers were scoffed at by the male-dominated scientific community at large. They were called "Pickering's Harem," because history can't go two minutes without being a misogynistic dipshit.

As she got deeper into the work, Annie realized that the current classification system for stars sucked. In Annie's day, all stars were lumped into groups of A, B, and C, which was helpful not at all because there are way more than three types. Much like there are more than four kinds of students at Hogwarts (brave, smart, evil, and miscellaneous), there are far more kinds of stars than there were categories to sort them into. So what's a girl to do? Make her own science rules.

Annie came up with the classification system of O, B, A, F, G, K, M, R, N, S, which was much more helpful and thorough. By 1910, Annie's system had become the worldwide standard, and, with minor modifications, remains so to this day.

Annie was freakishly good at star classification—she could do three stars a minute. In her lifetime, she classified more than three hundred and fifty thousand stars.

Her nickname among her squad became "The Census Taker of the Sky."

"IN THESE DAYS OF GREAT TROUBLE AND UNREST, IT IS GOOD TO HAVE SOMETHING OUTSIDE OUR OWN PLANET, SOMETHING FINE AND DISTANT AND COMFORTING TO TROUBLED MINDS. LET PEOPLE LOOK TO THE STARS."

In her copious free time, Annie was a photographer, and she published a photo book that was distributed at the Chicago World's Fair in 1893.

In addition to her earned degrees, Annie was awarded honorary degrees from all over the world, most notably from Oxford University. She was the first woman to be granted one.

The final leg of Annie's career was spent as curator of Astronomical Photographs at Harvard, living in a house in Cambridge she named Star Cottage (which is so magical and charming I can't even). Annie died in 1941, in Cambridge, Massachusetts. If ever there were a lady who should have been immortalized with a constellation, 'twas she.

The alleged story of how Pickering ended up hiring an astronomy girl squad is worth noting: As the story goes, he got so fed up with a male grad student being a dumbass that he hired his maid to do the student's work. He thought it would make a point that even she could do better. Turns out the maid was a genius and legit better than the boys. After that, Pickering hired only women for his astronomy team at Harvard. Pickering was a cool dude.

The mnemonic device for remembering Annie's classification, which is still taught today, is, "Oh, be a fine girl, kiss me right now, sweet," which is hysterically sexist, considering who came up with it.

CLELIA DUEL MOSHER

1863–1940, UNITED STATES

The Sex Positive Doctor Who Put Women's Health First

You know the old saying, "Where there's a Victorian lady, there's bound to be a fainting couch."

That is not a saying.

But it could have been, because the nineteenth century was lousy with swooning women who seemed inclined to faint at the smallest excitement. Most everyone at the time thought this was because women were simply physically inferior to men. Their poor woman bodies just couldn't handle the strain of daily living.

Everyone except Clelia Duel Mosher, sex-positive hulk-smasher of Victorian stereotypes about female fragility.

Clelia's fascination with human physiology began at an early age, and it was not only encouraged but also actively fostered by her father, Dr. Cornelius Mosher, a man with the appropriate amount of respect for women's education. He encouraged his daughter to read literary works and attend theatrical performances, and he built her a little greenhouse laboratory to explore her interest in botany. #DadGoals

Clelia was, to put it Victorian-ly, a sickly youth, and, as pro-education as her father was, he wasn't keen on Clelia going to college for fear of how it would affect her health. But Clelia used some of her heretofore wasted youthful rebellion and left home against her father's wishes to enroll at Wellesley College, as a twenty-five-year-old freshman. She eventually earned a degree in zoology before going on to study at Johns Hopkins Medical School, where her thesis was probably titled something like "Females Are Strong As Hell."

Allow me, if you will, to re-create her thesis defense.

Clelia: You know how women are physically inferior to men?

Board of Men: Ya, totes, they're so inferior.

Clelia: LIES. Women's bodies are literally just as competent as male bodies. You know how women are frail and can't breathe?

Board of Men: Ya, totes, so delicate.

Clelia: LIES. It's 'cause they're wearing effing corsets!

Clelia's medical school research was all about disproving the myth of female fragility and laying the blame where it belonged—on things like corsets. Shockingly, the fact that women might be constantly collapsing because fashion required them to constrict their waists to cartoonish proportions that made sandwiches of their internal organs had not been considered.

Clelia graduated from Johns Hopkins in 1900 and ran her own medical practice before becoming an assistant professor of personal hygiene at Stanford University. The main focus of her research was menstruation.

You think it's a taboo subject now? Time travel back to Victorian America and try to talk to someone about tampons.

Clelia gathered data from two thousand women over twelve thousand menstrual cycles. She then turned that data into science and used that science to help break the unhygienic habits and dispel the myths that could cause pain and infection during a woman's period. She also created a regimen of breathing exercises, called "Moshering," to relieve cramps, making her possibly the first American physician to specifically target menstrual cramp pain reduction (about damn time).

Clelia's most famous work, published posthumously, was a survey on my favorite euphemism ever, "Marital Relations." It's the only known existing survey from the time of American women's sex lives.

Surprise!—her research was controversial because it was frank, sex-positive, and advocated using "male sheaths" (second favorite euphemism—that's Victorian for condoms). Before this, research on sex in the United States had been done by men, and their conclusions were that women have no sexual desires and sex was only for reproduction. Clelia's work, which involved collecting data for more than thirty years, proved that most women were far from the sexually repressed proper ladies we think of now. Women could love and want sex as much as men did.

"BEHIND HER VIGOROUS EXTERIOR, CONTEMPORARIES REMEMBER . . . HER WILLINGNESS TO CONFRONT SYSTEMATICALLY THE ROLE OF SEXUALITY IN WOMEN."

Carl Degler

When she wasn't being a sex-positive period superhero, Clelia was a nurse in France during World War I and helped relocate and care for refugees. During her limited personal wartime leave, she worked as an extra set of hands in the post office, because she wanted to make sure the soldiers got their letters from home as fast as possible. My heart.

After she retired, Clelia wrote (tragically unpublished) romance novels and, shortly before her death at age seventy-seven, an (also tragically unpublished) autobiography, which she called *The Autobiography of a Happy Old Woman*.

Which is so sweet I'm getting a cavity.

SARAH BREEDLOVE
AKA MADAM C. J. WALKER

1867–1919, UNITED STATES

Boss Lady at the Head of a Hair Care Empire

At age seven, Sarah Breedlove was an orphan working in the Mississippi cotton fields.

At age twenty-one, she was a widowed single mother working for one dollar a day.

By age thirty-seven, she was a millionaire.

record scratch

You're probably wondering how she got there. Let me explain.

But first, let's talk about hair care and hygiene in nineteenth-century America. In summation, it was not great. Due to a lack of general understanding of hygiene (wut is vitamin?), hair products at the time contained crap like lye (and also sometimes literal crap), and most people did not have full heads of luscious, shampoo-commercial hair.

Anything that was bad for white women was way, way worse for black women, and hair care was no exception.

Sarah, like many black women, started losing her hair when she was in her twenties. And as the daughter of former slaves, an orphan, and a single mother living in poverty, she had enough to worry about without her hair falling out in chunks. Sarah began to search for a product to help combat her hair loss, but she couldn't find one. Because, to the surprise of no one, there were few hair products for black people in late nineteenth-century America. Especially for black women.

"There's got to be a better way!" cried Sarah, and she set out to create a line of quality hair products specifically for black women.

For years, while working for pennies at her brother's barbershop, Sarah studied hair care and natural remedies. She worked for rival hair care companies to learn their secrets. She taught herself about business.

And then, BAM! Sarah began selling Madam C. J. Walker's Wonderful Hair Grower, a scalp conditioning and healing formula for black women.

And it. Worked. Great.

Because Shark Tank was not yet a thing, Sarah, aka Madam C. J. Walker (a name she took on after her second marriage to a man named Charles Joseph Walker), traveled through the South selling her products door to door. The demand was enormous. Probably because it was the only good hair care product for black women at the time and made by a black woman to boot. Shrewd businesswoman that she was, Sarah increased the range of products she made—shampoos and powders and hair growth formulas, oh my!

With her daughter as her second in command, she expanded her business to Jamaica, Cuba, Costa Rica, Panama, and Haiti, employing thousands of black women around the world to manufacture her hair care products. By 1910, Sarah's was the largest African American-owned business in the country and she was a millionaire.

But was Sarah content to settle down with her fortune? No ma'am. She had a mission— to help more black women, and not just with their hair.

Sarah and her daughter built a factory in Indianapolis to manufacture their hair products, along with a hair salon and training school. There, Sarah trained saleswomen and gave them opportunities to support themselves in a way that was not available to many black women in turn-of-the-century America. Sarah organized the Hair Culturists Union of America convention, one of the first national meetings of businesswomen in United States history.

"I HAVE BUILT MY OWN FACTORY ON MY OWN GROUND."

Through this convention and her schools, Sarah encouraged women who worked for her not only to learn about business but also to be active in politics. The best way Sarah inspired political activism in women and helped build up black communities? She set the example. When a white mob murdered thirty-five black men, Sarah joined a group who visited the White House to advocate for anti-lynching legislation. She also donated tons of money to fund a black YMCA in Indiana, helping create a safe space for people of color in the city where her factory was located.

Basically, Sarah was all about using her success to help and elevate and create opportunities for other black people.

When she died in 1919, Sarah was the wealthiest black woman in America and the first female self-made millionaire in American history.

One hundred years later, her products are still for sale.

EDITH GARRUD

1872–1971, ENGLAND

The Jujitsu Suffragette

Imagine, if you will, you are a suffragette in turn-of-the-century England, attending a rally for the cause.

Police are prowling, smacking their palms with truncheons and looking for any excuse to use them to push around corseted, big-skirted, defenseless suffragettes.

But when those truncheons connect with your midsection, they bounce back. And then, out of nowhere, KAPOW! You whip a bowling pin out from under your voluminous Edwardian skirts and use it to pummel the police into a nearby floral arrangement, where your friends have previously placed razor wire to turn said floral arrangements into gaping jaws of carnage.

You have just opened up a can of suffrajitsu in the face of police brutality.

And it's all thanks to Edith Garrud.

Edith burst into the world in 1872 in Somerset, England, a baby born out of wedlock at a time when people could get tetchy about that sort of thing. As a young woman, she made friends with Edward William Barton-Wright, inventor of the martial art style known as Bartitsu. Bartitsu is a combination of stick fighting, bare-knuckled boxing, French savate, and Jujitsu and is most famous today for being Sherlock Holmes's fighting style of choice.

Little Edith (literally little—at her tallest, she stood 4'11" saw these mustachioed men elegantly brutalizing each other, decided that was a thing she would like to learn how to do, and enlisted William to teach her Bartitsu.

And when she had mastered it, she only wanted more.

Edith traveled from Wales, where she grew up, to London to study Tokyo-style Jujitsu with Sadakazu Uyenishi, the first Jujitsu master to teach outside of Japan. She took to it with the same exuberant talent as she had for Bartitsu, and by 1907, Edith was a thirty-five-year-old martial arts master who choreographed and starred in the first martial arts film made in the United Kingdom.

"But Mackenzi," you say, "get to the suffragettes!"

So it's 1908. The suffrage movement in England is reaching critical mass, and the police are getting brutal because they thought girls just wanted to have fun, but it turns out they actually want to have fundamental human rights.

What's a girl like Edith to do when she sees women beaten in the street by men twice their size just for asking for the right to vote? Open a Jujitsu school to teach suffragettes to unleash their feminine fury on the men standing in their way.

In her women-only gyms, Edith taught the suffragettes martial arts to defend themselves against police brutality. She also assembled an elite hell-raising, face-breaking girl gang of thirty women to protect Emmeline Pankhurst and other leaders of the movement. Edith personally trained these fighting girlfriends in hand to hand combat and outfitted them with weapons they could conceal under their skirts and armor to wear under their dresses. Once their training was complete, she sent her Jujitsu suffragettes to the streets to defend the frontlines of their movement.

That's really what they were called. The Jujitsu suffragettes. Where's that in the Mary Poppins song?

Edith trained the Jujitsu suffragettes, but she also organized decoys and tools of evasion. She would vouch for suffragettes when they needed an alibi, saying they'd been at her dojo when really they'd been out hurling Molotov cocktails at mailboxes. She did all this while also teaching classes where women learned Edith's signature move—flipping cops over her shoulder and smashing them to the ground.

"NOT A MAN IS GOING TO PROTECT ME, BECAUSE THIS IS A WOMAN'S FIGHT, AND WE ARE GOING TO PROTECT OURSELVES!"

The women's suffrage movement piped down during World War I, but Edith continued teaching women to defend themselves. Later in life she was asked to give demonstrations to London police officers who wanted to use her cop-flipping technique against rapscallions and ne're-do-wells. Edith also worked as a fight choreographer for stage and film and was the first female martial arts teacher in the Western world.

Edith died in 1971, at age ninety-nine. In her last interview, she offered the reporter the recipe she'd just used for her birthday cake.

It's worth noting that the early suffrage movement in the Western world had issues, because it only recognized white women's rights. This was typical of the time period—it's no excuse, but it's historical context. Intersectionality wasn't always a thing that occurred to the white ladies waving the banners and throwing themselves in front of the king's carriage. However, while the suffrage movement was often problematic due to its lack of inclusivity, it's worth talking about because it paved the way for universal suffrage for women of all races.

Turn-of-the-century suffragettes didn't just want the vote: They were also petitioning for their right to divorce and inherit land.

Tangentially related but mostly just cool, turn-of-the-century women used to have Jujitsu parties, in the same way Tupperware parties and Paint Bar Nights are a thing now. First rule of Jujitsu party? Don't talk about Jujitsu party.

EMMY NOETHER

1882–1935, GERMANY

Theoretically, the Most Important Woman in Physics

When Einstein calls you the most significant and creative woman in the history of mathematics, you can probably call it a day and go home.

Unless you're Emmy Noether, whose pursuit of game-changing innovation in the field of numbers was, in a word, tenacious.

Emmy's early aspirations were to teach English and French at girls' schools in early-twentieth-century Germany, where she was born and raised. You've probably already guessed that that didn't happen. Before she started teaching, she had a major change of heart and decided she'd rather study mathematics in the tradition of her father, self-taught mathematician Max Noether. In Germany at that time, women weren't allowed to enroll in university-level math classes—they could only audit with the permission of the professor. So Emmy spent two years auditing classes at the University of Erlangen, in her hometown, receiving no credit and no degree. Luckily she did so well on the exams that the university ended up granting her a bachelor's degree anyway. She went on to receive a PhD there, with a dissertation on algebraic invariants.

After graduating, in order to find employment in her field of expertise, Emmy had to work at the university without pay or a title for seven years—basically the unpaid internship from hell. But all the while, between grading papers and holding office hours, she worked on her own research, primarily in abstract algebra (a new field at the time), which involved things like structures and rings and groups and why they behave the way they do.

In 1915, Emmy was invited to the University of Göttingen, where she had done some postgraduate work, to help explain Einstein's theories, using math from her dissertation, to the students and staff. There were loud protests about a woman joining the faculty—and not only a woman but a Jewish woman in right-before-World War II Germany, so she wasn't exactly a first-round draft pick—though a lot of her mathematical colleagues, including Einstein himself, made a fierce case for her employment. One, David Hilbert, said, "I do not see that the sex of the candidate is an argument against her. . . . After all, we are a university, not a bathhouse." Emmy was granted permission to lecture, but—because sexism never rests—only under the name of the male professors who had invited her, and she still didn't have a salary, which is really taking this whole wage gap thing to the extreme.

For the next several years, Emmy continued her research on abstract algebra, specifically developing her groundbreaking Noether's theorem, which basically states that wherever you find some symmetry, you'll also find a corresponding law of conservation. I don't totally understand this, but I am told by my sources that it united two conceptual pillars of physics, symmetry in nature and the laws of conservation, and that was important. Noether's theorem is considered as important as Einstein's theory of relativity in the study of modern physics and algebra—it's still the foundation of many modern scientific advancements (like the hunt for the Higgs boson). Some physicists even make a strong case that Emmy's theorem is the backbone of modern physics.

"SHE TAUGHT US TO THINK IN SIMPLE, AND THUS GENERAL, TERMS AND NOT IN COMPLICATED ALGEBRAIC CALCULATION."

P. S. Alexandroff

Emmy was so obsessed with math she didn't have time for much else. She left behind few personal papers or written records of her life and never married or mentioned any romantic trysts. She didn't care for housework or appearance—she was known for keeping her hair long and unruly, and it often fell out of its half-hearted arrangements as she bounced around her classroom excitedly talking about numbers.

But aside from being a brilliant mathematician, Emmy was a Jew, a pacifist, and a woman—a dangerous combination in Weimar Germany. In 1933, she was denied permission to teach by the Nazi government. Since it was looking too dangerous for her to stay in Germany, she accepted a guest professorship at Bryn Mawr College in Pennsylvania (for which she was recommended by Einstein, which, I would imagine, is the sort of employment reference that makes you a shoo-in). She lived there for eighteen months, until she died in 1935, at age fifty-three.

Beyond her boss-ass theorem, Emmy's research fundamentally changed the way mathematicians approach their work. She pioneered a conceptual approach to algebra that led to principles that connected algebra, geometry, linear algebra, topology, and logic.

And while I might not know what most of that means, I'm pretty sure it's awesome.

ALICE BALL

1892–1916, UNITED STATES

Leprosy Meets Its Match

We had a cure for leprosy for centuries. This crippling disease that, for thousands of years, left millions with painful deformities and ostracized from society worldwide could have been wiped out for good with oil from one plant.

And we knew it. We just couldn't make it work.

Until Alice Ball came along.

Alice was born in Seattle, Washington, in 1892. Her family was on the upper end of middle class—her grandfather was one of the first African American daguerreotype photographers, and her father carried on that legacy as a photographer and newspaper editor.

But Alice was a STEM girl at heart. She attended the University of Washington, where she earned degrees in both pharmaceutical chemistry and pharmacy, before going to the University of Hawaii to earn a master's in chemistry, the first woman and the first black person in the institution's history awarded a higher degree.

But back to leprosy.

It's a little bastard. And for most of history, if you developed the disease, your life was basically over. In turn-of-the-century America, people found to have leprosy were forcibly removed from their homes and confined to remote leper colonies, and that was about as good a situation as you could hope for anywhere in the world.

Around 1300, the Chinese discovered that oil extracted from the chaulmoogra tree could be used to fight leprosy. But as helpful as this information was, the oil was in the wrong form, and no one could figure out how to do anything with it. Topically applied, it showed some healing results, but it didn't penetrate the skin deep enough to get much done. Taken orally, it was more effective but gave patients crippling nausea. When injected, the oil would stick together and turn skin into bloody bubble wrap. On patients who already had leprosy.

How could we get the oil to circulate through the body? The entire world wondered this for basically six hundred years.

And then Alice Ball wrote her thesis.

Alice developed a process to isolate the ethyl esters of the fatty acids in chaulmoogra oil so that they could be injected painlessly and travel deep enough below the skin to fight the disease. She had found a way to make the cure into a cure. People suffering from leprosy who had been dealing with constant, painful injections of chaulmoogra oil that weren't really doing anything were cured. Thousands of people around the world suddenly found their death sentences rescinded. They got their lives back.

Alice's research was cut tragically short when she died at age twenty-four, in 1916, most likely from accidental exposure to chlorine gas. Arthur L. Dean, the president of the University of Hawaii at the time, continued her work. But don't get too excited—he published it without giving Alice any credit and instead took all the glory for himself. He even had the nerve to rename the technique the Dean Method, which is just the icing on the douche cake. Thank goodness Alice's thesis advisor, Dr. Harry T. Hollman, called him out. The method was re-renamed the Ball Method and was used into the 1940s, when leprosy-fighting antibiotics were developed.

"ALICE BALL WAS BRILLIANT, AND WENT FAR IN CHEMISTRY."

John Pratt

Today, the lone chaulmoogra tree on the University of Hawaii campus bears a plaque with Alice Ball's name.

DOROTHY ARZNER

1897–1979, UNITED STATES

Lights! Camera! Feminism!

Dorothy Arzner didn't grow up in California—she grew up in Hollywood, which is a different place entirely. On the outskirts of Beverly Hills, her parents ran a restaurant where all the big silent film stars would hang out and eat greasy food and complain about contracts and costumes and costars. Dorothy was raised on familiar terms with the business of making moving pictures.

In 1919, Dorothy started as a stenographer at Famous Players-Lasky Corporation, which became Paramount Pictures in 1930. Her super glamorous job was typing up scripts. But part of the Hollywood success story is clawing your way up from the mailroom, or, in this case, the script office. And by nothing but moxie and bootstraps, Dorothy was soon promoted to film editing—she cut fifty films for Paramount before being promoted again, this time to writing.

Dorothy knew what she wanted, and what she wanted was to be in charge. She wanted to be a director, and when Paramount refused to give her that position, she threatened to walk out and take her brilliant brain elsewhere. Paramount changed their tune, and Dorothy became the only female director working in Hollywood at the time.

Her first film was *Fashions for Women*, a silent movie about a cigarette girl who impersonates a Parisian fashion model and hijinks ensue. And it was a hit! Or, at least, a hit-adjacent. Enough of a hit that Paramount gave Dorothy another picture to direct. And then another. And another. Until eventually she landed her biggest picture yet: *The Wild Party*.

The Wild Party starred Clara Bow, a silent film actress and 1930s it girl—literally (the phrase "it girl" was coined for her). Clara had an expressive face and giant anime eyes that had served her well in silent films, but the movies were talking now, and Clara had seen many of her fellow stars collapse under the weight of having to deliver lines while acting. When she stepped onto the set of *The Wild Party*, her first talkie, she was freaked out.

So freaked out that she had a bad habit of breaking character midscene to look right at the hidden mics. Which rather shattered the fourth wall.

Instead of Lina Lamont–ing her leading lady and strapping a mic to a big-ass corsage over her cleavage, Dorothy leapt up from her director's chair to do some on-set problem solving. She tied a mic to a fishing pole and hung it above Clara, so her star didn't have to worry about where she had to direct her lines as she moved around the set.

"IF ONE WAS GOING TO BE IN THE MOVIE BUSINESS, ONE SHOULD BE A DIRECTOR BECAUSE HE WAS THE ONE WHO TOLD EVERYONE ELSE WHAT TO DO."

Too bad she didn't slap a patent on it, because Dorothy is credited with inventing the first boom mic.

Dorothy was the first woman to join the Directors Guild of America, with a resume of overtly feminist films featuring Strong Female Characters. I don't know if you've watched a lot of films from the 1930s (or recent years, for that matter) but this wasn't common. On the set of her film *Craig's Wife*, Dorothy took misogynistic source material about a poor, defenseless man trapped in a marriage with a frigid wife and turned it into a plea for women to be considered their own people rather than the beautiful possessions of men. Her film *Dance, Girl, Dance* featured an iconic scene where a female dancer shuts down her male hecklers by yelling back at them.

Dorothy's films helped launch the careers of actresses like Katharine Hepburn, Lucille Ball, Joan Crawford, and Rosalind Russell. In a male-dominated industry, she made movies starring women, about women helping women, which helped launch the careers of women. Be still my heart.

Aside from being the sort of feminist you can't miss, the gal pals in Dorothy's films were often subtextually queer. Sometimes textually. The two leading ladies in *Dance, Girl, Dance* were described by a modern reviewer as "tiffing and dancing like a crypto-lesbian Fred and Ginger." So. Sign me up.

This was most likely because Dorothy herself was a butch lesbian who wore men's clothes and kept her hair cut short. She romanced many a beautiful actress (like any self-respecting Hollywood dynamo), including Billie Burke, who played Glinda in The *Wizard of Oz*. For the last forty years of her life, Dorothy lived with her long-term partner, choreographer Marion Morgan.

Dorothy directed her last film, *First Comes Courage*, in 1943, but due to illness, she was forced to abandon the project. She never returned to the city of stars, but she kept directing. Her projects later in life spanned from Women's Army Corps training videos during World War II to Pepsi commercials with her pal Joan Crawford.

In the 1960s, Dorothy began teaching at UCLA's film school. One of her mentees was a little wide-eyed nobody you've probably never heard of named Francis Ford Coppola.

Dorothy died in 1979. With sixteen feature directing credits to her name—and more uncredited—she remains Hollywood's most prolific female director. You can find her star on the Hollywood Walk of Fame in the 1500 block of Vine Street. Leave a boom mic in her honor.

NWANYERUWA

TWENTIETH CENTURY, NIGERIA

Leader of the Igbo Women's War

1929 was a rough year.

The Great Depression had its teeth in America, and the effects were being felt all over the world. In Nwanyeruwa's home country of Nigeria, the financial collapse in America had driven down the price of Nigerian exports. The British were still hoarding large chunks of Africa, including Nigeria, and calling it their own, but they were struggling with money, too.

So the British decided to start taxing women in Nigeria, which they had never done before. This was an easy motion to get passed, because Nigerian women had little to no say in anything. You might remember another British colony that was opposed to taxation without representation from its oppressive rulers. It was the same sort of thing.

Like many women in the country, Nwanyeruwa was furious over this. She was also brave enough to call out the British on how grossly unfair it was. And she was almost strangled by the tax collector as a result. But don't worry—when he grabbed her throat, she grabbed his right back. Her cries for help brought another of her husband's wives running and together they fought the tax collector off.

Nwanyeruwa reported the tax collector to his boss, a British-appointed warrant chief named Okugo, who literally used "are you sure you weren't asking for it?" as an excuse to ignore her complaint.

If you're anything like me, you're probably vibrating with rage at this point. So was Nwanyeruwa. She decided to do something about it.

That something was staging a giant sit in/dance party/women's march in protest of British taxation.

Nwanyeruwa rallied the women in her village, and they all camped out in front of Okugo's house. They played music and danced and made up songs about how dumb he was that they sang loudly when he was home.

Okugo went ballistic. He attacked the women—stabbed one with a spear, shot an arrow through another, and eventually set his house on fire and blamed the protestors. But Nwanyeruwa was undaunted.

She had the women of her village behind her. And they were going to shove inequality where the sun doesn't shine.

Nwanyeruwa's movement began to spread to other towns around Nigeria. Women across the country began protesting against taxation without representation and also the fact that a bunch of white British dudes had no right to be in their country and taking their money in the first place. They took to the streets. They marched while singing, ignoring the men who claimed they were just being hysterical. They persisted. They resisted.

Eventually, some groups of the march became more militant, though they never harmed anyone. Instead they cut telegraph wires, vandalized European institutions, and freed prisoners from jail. It was the British who got violent in response. They started running female protesters over with their cars. They opened fire onto the protesters. They burned villages.

The conflict was known as the Igbo Women's War, though it was only a violent war on the side of the British. Nwanyeruwa and her marching ladies did no harm. They just wanted representation and equality.

Eventually, the British relented. Taxation on women was withdrawn and asshat warrant chiefs like Okugo had their powers limited. We don't know what happened to Nwanyeruwa, but what we can say for sure is that her refusal to accept injustice kicked off one of the first major challenges to British authority in Africa. One woman's refusal to accept unrelenting colonial oppression started a movement that became thousands strong and helped end centuries of colonial injustice in Africa.

Who said women marching never got us anywhere?

RUKMINI DEVI ARUNDALE

1904–1986, INDIA

Why Walk When You Can Dance?

When Anna Pavlova says you should study dance, it's like J. K. Rowling advising you to write a book. And in spite of being thirty years old, an age at which most ballerinas are retiring, and having no previous dance experience, Rukmini Devi Arundale took that advice to heart. Though, neither she nor Anna Pavlova likely could have anticipated that that first ballet class would lead to Rukmini revitalizing a traditional form of Indian dance that was on the brink of dying out.

Rukmini was born in 1904 in Madurai, a city-state in southern India. She was raised in a household that practiced theosophy, a collection of mystical and occultist philosophies that seek knowledge of the nature of divinity and the origin and purpose of the universe. Rukmini grew up hearing these ideas both from her father and their family friend Annie Besant, one of the founders of theosophy. When Rukmini married a theosophy missionary, she traveled with him and Annie around the world, spreading their messages.

Which is when Rukmini fell in love with dance. Dance of every kind. She met Anna Pavlova and developed a hardcore woman crush on her after watching her perform. Anna encouraged Rukmini to study ballet and to seek inspiration in the classical dances of India as she developed her own style.

In her search for those signature moves, Rukmini discovered sadhir, India's oldest classical dance style. But sadhir was dying out. Its exclusively female practitioners had historically been temple courtesans, which caused a stigma around performing it in public. It was forbidden by the colonial British dummies who took over India, and anyone who wanted to learn it was considered low and vulgar.

Rukmini was going to change that.

Her first step was rebranding. She created a new name for the dance, Bharatanatyam. Then she introduced musical instruments, designed costumes and jewelry specifically for dancers of Bharatanatyam, established set and lighting design elements, and developed dance-dramas based on Indian epics and mythology. These changes revamped the dance style and brought it into the twentieth century.

In 1935, Rukmini gave her first public performance of Bharatanatyam, and within a year, she and her husband had established an academy of dance and music for teenagers in India. She is considered the most important revivalist of classical Indian dance and instrumental in reestablishing traditional Indian arts and crafts.

"MANY PEOPLE HAVE SAID MANY THINGS. I CAN ONLY SAY I DID NOT CONCIOUSLY GO AFTER DANCE. IT FOUND ME."

When she wasn't dancing like no one was watching her save a nearly forgotten cultural dance, Rukmini was an animal rights activist, vegetarianism advocate, and founder of a center that taught an ancient Indian method of textile printing, which had been dying out just like Bharatanatyam.

In 1977, the prime minister of India offered to nominate her for the role of president of India, but she turned it down. It wouldn't have left her enough time to dance.

MARIYA OKTYABRSKAYA

1905–1944, RUSSIA

Smashing Nazis in a Tank of Her Own

Mariya Oktyabrskaya started her life as a poster child for the post-Russian Revolution communist regime: Born into dirt-eating levels of poverty, she participated in the Russian Revolution, married a Red Army soldier, and joined the cause as a telephone operator working for whatever minimum wage was in 1930s Russia.

Everything changed when the German nation attacked.

In 1941, Germany cruised into the Motherland and began shelling out mortars and turning anyone who got in their way into toe jam between the treads of their steel-plated war machines. Being a soldier, Mariya's husband went to war. Being a good communist housewife, Mariya stayed home and hated the Nazis from a distance.

Until she received word that her husband had died in battle.

At which point Mariya transformed into a concentrated beam of white-knuckled Nazi-hating nuclear rage.

Mariya sold everything she owned and used the money to buy a big-ass brand-new 26-ton T-34 Main Battle Tank. A tank that she learned to drive herself. A tank that she named Fighting Girlfriend.

Mariya then wrote to Joseph Stalin, *"My husband was killed in action defending the motherland. I want revenge on the fascist dogs for his death and for the death of Soviet people tortured by the fascist barbarians. For this purpose I've deposited all my personal savings . . . in order to build a tank. I kindly ask to name the tank 'Fighting Girlfriend' and to send me to the frontline as a driver of said tank."*

TL;DR: "Me and Fighting Girlfriend want to blow up Nazis."

To which Stalin replied, "Welcome aboard."

Mariya was assigned to the 26th Guards Tank Brigade, an elite band of the Russian military. The men of said brigade didn't quite know what to make of the rampaging warrior woman vibrating with revenge and a tank of her own, so they decided the best thing to do would be to throw her into the front lines and see what happened.

What happened is that Mariya and Fighting Girlfriend freaking crushed it.

In her first battle, Mariya stole a move straight out of *The Fast and the Furious* and plowed Fighting Girlfriend into the path of the oncoming Nazi tanks, and then hit the gas. She and her tank crew were the first tank to breach the German position. Afterward, she wrote home to her sister, "I've had my baptism by fire. I beat the bastards. Sometimes I'm so angry I can't even breathe."

For the next year, Mariya continued to drive her armored-whale of a death machine over the Nazis with the sort of suicidal abandon that can only be called ferocious. In her most famous incident, Mariya leaped from Fighting Girlfriend in the middle of a battle to do repairs on the tread. It seems debatable who Mariya loved more—the husband for whom she had sworn revenge or the tank with which she extracted it.

Mariya, who was promoted to sergeant for her bravery, and Fighting Girlfriend took part in the largest tank battle in history, the Battle of Kursk, which helped turn the tide of the war away from Hitler once and for all.

After a year on the frontlines, Mariya was killed in battle. The Germans were on the retreat, and the Russians were eager to help them retreat by driving their asses back to Berlin. Of course, Mariya was at the head of this charge, when, during a night raid, she was struck with shrapnel while trying to fix her darling Fighting Girlfriend in the thick of the fight.

Upon her death, she received the Hero of the Soviet Union award for bravery, the highest award a soldier could receive.

Though I picked Mariya to highlight, there are A LOT of women who served in the Russian army during World War II who were just as badass. The history of women in combat in Russia is rich, especially during World War II, but almost entirely forgotten.

IRENA SENDLER

1910–2008, POLAND

Rescuer of the Jewish Children of Warsaw

Irena Sendler knew how to be a good ally.

Though her family wasn't Jewish, her father was a doctor with mostly Jewish patients in Warsaw, Poland, and he taught Irena from an early age to stand up for history's most stepped-on religious community. As a young woman, Irena studied literature at Warsaw University, but never got her degree, because she was expelled. For making lots of noise about the fact that Jewish students were forced to sit separately from students of other faiths. On brand.

And when Irena saw Hitler coming, she got in the way.

When the Germans began to force Polish Jews to move their families into the Warsaw Ghetto, Irena used her connections as an employee of the Social Welfare Department to create false papers for more than three thousand Jewish families to protect them from relocation. Remember: Giving any kind of assistance to Jews in German-occupied Poland was punishable by death, for both the helper and their family.

But tiny (literally tiny, because she was 4'11"), Irena looked death in the eyes and laughed—presumably to create a distraction while she saved Jews.

Despite the efforts of Irena and many others, 450,000 Jews still ended up behind the hellish walls of the Warsaw Ghetto, a space the size of Central Park. A quarter of the Jews forced into the ghetto died from starvation and disease before deportation to concentration camps even began.

But instead of giving up because she was just one person, Irena rolled up her sleeves and got to work.

Irena became involved with the Żegota (a Polish underground group that assisted Jews) and was asked to head up their children's division. This didn't mean she was in charge of a squad of kid rebels, though that would be awesome. This meant she was in charge of getting Jewish kids out of the ghetto. Which is actually even more awesome.

As an employee of the Social Welfare Department, Irena was one of the few non-Jews in Warsaw with permission to enter the ghetto. The Nazis were certain Jews were filthy, diseased subhumans carrying all manner of germs, and they were petrified those germs would spread outside the ghetto, so they employed women like Irena to go behind the walls, check for signs of diseases like typhus, and make sure the sickness remained contained.

Except Irena was actually using this job as a ploy to smuggle Jewish children out of the ghetto and place them with Christian families right under Nazi noses.

Irena came up with increasingly creative ways to get kids out of the ghetto, past the Nazis stationed at the entrance and throughout Warsaw, and to safety. She smuggled babies and small children in ambulances, in trams, and through sewer pipes, and hid them in packages, suitcases, sacks, and toolboxes. She trained a dog to sit in the front seat of her ambulance with her and bark to drown out the children's cries. 12/10, would pet.

In 1943, Irena was arrested by the Gestapo and tortured for information about her resistance network, but she refused to betray any of her Żegota squad or the children they rescued.

She never gave them anything.

As a result, Irena had both her legs broken by her interrogators and was sentenced to death by firing squad. But the Żegota swept in for a glorious rescue mission. They bribed Irena's guards and, on the way to her execution, she was able to escape.

After her imprisonment, Irena returned to Warsaw under a fake name and continued her involvement with the Żegota. She got a job as a nurse and hid Jews in the hospital where she worked until the end of the war,

when the Germans turned tail and scurried out of Poland with Russia on their heels.

Over the course of the war, Irena saved more than 2,500 Jewish children from the Warsaw Ghetto. That's twice as many as Oskar Schindler, of Spielberg film fame. She wrote the name of every child she and her network saved on pieces of cigarette paper, put them in glass jars, and buried them in her backyard. This was done in the hope that someday, she would be able to reunite these children with their families.

Because the anti-Semitic communist party took over in Poland after World War II, Irena received no recognition for her efforts. Instead, she was imprisoned *again* and her work forgotten. Knowledge of her heroism is mostly credited to a group of high school students and their National History Day project about her in 1999. Irena has since received the Order of the White Eagle, was named Humanitarian of the Year, and was made an honorary citizen of Israel, among other accolades.

In 2007, Irena was up for the Nobel Peace Prize, but she was not selected.

Al Gore won instead, for a PowerPoint presentation about weather.

Just kidding, climate change is real and important, and Al Gore, Imma let you finish, but IRENA SENDLER WAS ONE OF THE GREATEST WOMEN OF ALL TIME.

Irena died in 2008, at age ninety-eight. She lived in Warsaw her whole life.

URSULA NORDSTROM

1910–1988, UNITED STATES

Publisher of Good Books for Bad Children

Ursula Nordstrom was an unlikely candidate for revolutionizing children's literature in the twentieth century. She couldn't spell. She was bad at making decisions. She didn't go to college. She had no children of her own. When her nemesis, the New York Public Library's first children's librarian, Anne Carroll Moore, demanded to know what qualified Ursula to publish books for children, she replied, "Well, I am a former child, and I haven't forgotten a thing."

But if you have ever read to a child, or have been a child who was read to, it's almost certain you know her work.

With only a few business classes under her belt courtesy of the Scudder Preparatory School, Ursula's publishing career began in 1936, when she took a job at Harper & Brothers (today HarperCollins) as a clerk in the textbook department. She soon transferred to a position as an assistant in the division known as Harper Books for Boys and Girls.

In the age of *Harry Potter*, we don't think of the children's book as a new phenomenon, but in early-twentieth-century America, it was a growing field. The young readers departments at most publishing houses were small and run almost exclusively by women who had to deal daily with the sexist noise of male colleagues. Children's reading rooms, now a fixture in most libraries, were a new phenomenon beginning to spread across the country.

Prior to Ursula's reign at Harper, the children's books that did exist tended to skew one of two ways—bright, sunny tales where everything is shiny all the time because children are fragile and we must protect them from the ugly truth of the world, or moralistic tales in which there was always a grizzly lesson to be learned that comes at you like a sack of bricks.

Ursula changed that. In 1940, she was promoted to editor in chief of the Department of Books for Boys and Girls, and the books published during her tenure were different. They shunned sentimentality and the overly precious treatment of childhood and changed the tone of children's books to what we embrace today. Her goal was to create books that entertained kids but also related to their experiences, and part of that was acknowledging that children

often live on familiar terms with darkness and complexity in their everyday lives.

Under her command, the misfit crew of the understaffed, messy office of Harper's Books for Boys and Girls grew from three employees to almost forty and turned out some of the most influential and bestselling kid's books of all time. If you've read *Where the Wild Things Are, Harold and the Purple Crayon, Charlotte's Web, Julie of the Wolves, Danny and the Dinosaur, Where the Sidewalk Ends, Goodnight Moon, In the Night Kitchen, The Giving Tree, Runaway Bunny, Harriet the Spy,* or *Stuart Little,* you can thank Ursula.

"THE RIGID WORLD OF GOOD AND BAD IS INFINITELY EASIER TO WRITE ABOUT THAN THE REAL WORLD. BECAUSE THE WRITER OF BOOKS ABOUT THE REAL WORLD HAS TO DIG DEEP AND TELL TRUTHS."

As an editor, she published a lot of firsts in children's books, including the first young-adult novel to overtly mention homosexuality (*I'll Get There. It Better Be Worth the Trip,* by John Donovan, 1969), the first mention of menstruation in a kid's book (*The Long Secret,* by Louise Fitzhugh, 1965), one of the first novels for young readers about racism in contemporary America (*Call Me Charley,* by Jesse C. Jackson, 1945), and the first portrayal of full frontal nudity in a picture book (*In the Night Kitchen,* by Maurice

Sendak, 1970; a slightly more dubious first than the others, but still, it's indicative of the guts and gusto with which Ursula approached her books).

Ursula demanded a high caliber of work from her authors—her most notorious note left scribbled in the margins of manuscripts was N.G.E.F.Y., which stood for "Not Good Enough for You." On the flip side, when deserving, she doled out the sort of compliments that would have her authors glowing. She fought constantly with the higher-ups at Harper to be allocated the same resources for her department that others received.

She was also notorious (in a good way) for going to bat for her authors when their books were challenged for breaking the mold. She replied to letters written by teachers and librarians condemning the nudity in *In the Night Kitchen* with her trademark eloquence, wit, and shut-it-down-ness: "Should not those of us who stand between the creative artist and the child be very careful not to sift our reactions to such books through our own adult prejudices and neuroses?. . . It is only adults who ever feel threatened by Sendak's work." Her defense of a book by Ruth Kraus concluded, "Oh hell, it just boils down to: you just can't explain this sort of basic wonderful stuff to some adults."

Ursula was a special champion for queer children's literature, in a time when any whiff of homosexuality had to be aggressively subtextual. She herself wrote one of the first lesbian books for young readers, *The Secret Language*, and mentored queer authors, including Maurice Sendak, Margaret Wise Brown, Arnold Lobel, Louise Fitzhugh, and M. E. Kerr. Ursula lived with her longtime partner, Mary Griffith, who she met while working at Harper, for decades.

When Ursula was offered a "promotion" from the children's to the adult's department, she turned it down with the eloquent but mic-dropping statement, "I couldn't possibly be interested in books for dead dull finished adults, and thank you very much but I have to get back to my desk to publish some more good books for bad children." But, in 1960, she did take a job as vice president of Harper, the first woman to hold the position.

It took Ursula three attempts before she actually retired. When she stepped down as publisher at Harper, they gave her an eponymous imprint, Ursula Nordstrom Books, which ran until 1979, and after that, she continued to work as a consultant.

Ursula died in 1988 at the age of seventy-eight, Patron Saint of Childhood. The books she brought into the world during her time at Harper remain some of the bestselling books of all time.

For children or otherwise.

Ursula Nordstrom's letters have been collected by children's literature scholar Leonard S. Marcus and published in a book called *Dear Genius: The Letters of Ursula Nordstrom*. She's sassy, articulate, and brilliant in every one.

Ursula and Maurice Sendak are #relationshipgoals—I can't not mention their gorgeous friendship/mentorship. The two became acquainted when Maurice was working as a window dresser at the legendary New York City toy store FAO Schwarz (RIP), and Ursula recruited him from there to draw books for children. He spent several years illustrating other people's stories before he began working on his own books. The relationship between these two really shines through in their letters. In perhaps the sweetest interaction ever, Ursula wrote a letter shoring up a discouraged Maurice just before he started working on the book that would really put him on the map, *Where the Wild Things Are*. When Maurice bemoaned how he'd never write like Tolstoy, Ursula told him, "You may not be Tolstoy, but Tolstoy wasn't Sendak, either."

As previously mentioned, Ursula had a nemesis. But honestly, what outspoken broad with big ideas doesn't? Ursula's legendary feud was with Anne Carroll Moore, the first children's librarian at the New York Public Library, whose turned-up noses cost *Charlotte's Web* the Newbury Medal, the highest award for children's books. Ursula, much like an elephant, never forgot, and, like a vengeful she-beast, never forgave either. "Forgive me for talking stupidly today," she wrote in one of her letters. "I was at my worst, but I blame it on Anne Carroll Moore." Shady AF.

ELVIRA DE LA FUENTE CHAUDOIR

1913–1995, PERU, FRANCE, AND ENGLAND

Drinker, Gambler, Playgirl, Spy

Operation Fortitude was carried out by an unlikely squad of double agents in Britain who fed Germany incorrect information about the D-Day invasion during World War II. Their ranks included a bisexual Peruvian playgirl and gambler, a tiny Polish fighter pilot, a fast-talking Frenchwoman, a Serbian playboy, and a failed chicken farmer.

To be clear, I would donate to a Kickstarter for a misfit wartime Avengers-style espionage movie about them in a hot second.

But until that goes live, let's talk about the bisexual Peruvian playgirl, Elvira de la Fuente Chaudoir.

The child of a Peruvian fertilizer magnate working as an ambassador in Vichy France, Elvira, like many young women of history, had too much brain and not enough outlets. As a result, she spent most of her time entertaining herself by seeing how many commandments she could break in a single afternoon.

Educated, spoiled, and exceedingly rebellious, as soon as she was old enough, Elvira ran away from her parents and into the arms of a Belgian stockbroker. Their four years of tumultuous marriage ended after Elvira slept her way across Brussels (with both women and men—as one report later put it, "she favors the companionship of women who may not be careful of their virginity"). Known for bailing when things got sour, Elvira ran away again, this time to Cannes with her best friend, where they proceeded to raise hell as the Thelma and Louise of the French gaming tables.

Elvira wasn't particularly worried about her safety when the Germans invaded France—she was young, rich, and hot, so basically invincible. But she was also in debt—she never seemed to know when to hold 'em and when to fold 'em and as a result she'd racked up an impressive roster of gambling debts. The German invasion was a good excuse to flee to England and start a new life where her creditors couldn't catch her.

After a failed gig at the BBC, Elvira spent most of her time shuffling between the bars and the card tables, complaining to anyone who would listen about how she had

no money and was looking for something beyond bridge that would keep that big brain of hers occupied.

And the right person must have heard her, because she soon ended up interviewing with the head of MI6, who offered her a job with the British secret service.

Elvira had a few great traits for a spy: one, she had a Peruvian passport, which would allow her to travel in Europe in wartime, and her diplomat parents provided cover for her movements in occupied France. Two, she had a reputation as a cocktail grubbing party girl who cared for nothing beyond booze, betting, and batting for both teams. And three, she was broke as a joke, and MI6 paid better than losing at cards.

The plan was this: After training her up in the skills needed for sabotage, Elvira would be sent into France, where she would parade herself before the Germans as a tantalizing recruit for their war effort. Once the Third Reich had signed her on, she would report back to Britain from behind enemy lines and feed her German employers bogus information made up by MI6 about Allied movements.

And it worked. After just a few weeks in Cannes, Elvira made eyes at a dark-haired stranger across the bar who spoke French with a German accent, and soon not only had the Germans recruited her, but she also had a German salary going into her bridge antes.

Unbeknownst to her German employers, this officially made Elvira a member of XX, or the Double Cross, the team of English agents spying on the Germans from within their own ranks. Her codename was "Bronx," for her favorite drink.

Elvira wrote letters to the Germans filled with trivial girly details like "can I pull off a red lip" and "ten clothing items that make him lose interest," but in between the lines, she wrote information about British movements in invisible ink. Of course, it was all fake information from MI6, but the Third Reich didn't know that; they trusted her implicitly. Since the Germans knew an invasion was imminent, and since they considered Elvira one of their most reliable agents, she was tasked with sending them information via coded bank deposits about the time and location of the Allies' planned charge. Elvira told them the British were definitely going to come at them from the Bay of Biscay, and they should definitely move all their troops there.

Which, obviously, was fake news. But it worked.

When the Allies landed in Normandy, there was an entire tank division chilling in the Bay of Biscay, waiting for the attack. All thanks to Elvira.

Elvira spent the rest of her life running a souvenir shop and living off her inheritance. A month before her death, she received a five-thousand-pound check from MI6, a small token of thanks for her help in the war effort.

And probably lost it all at bridge before she breathed her last.

JACKIE MITCHELL

1913–1987, UNITED STATES

The Left-Handed Teen Who Struck Out Baseball's MVPs

Jackie Mitchell had the good fortune of being born one door down from baseball hall-of-fame pitcher Dazzy Vance, in Chattanooga, Tennessee. Dazzy noticed that the scrappy, left-handed tomboy next door had a good eye for America's favorite pastime and decided she was the one who would inherit his legendary fastball. Though I have a feeling no matter where she grew up, Jackie would have found her way onto the pitcher's mound eventually. She was basically born with a baseball glove on.

Armed with Vance's teaching, her parents' refusal to make her conform to gender norms regarding girls and sports, and a God-given talent, at age sixteen, Jackie began pitching for the Engelettes, a women's baseball team in Chattanooga. It's there she met Joe Engel, owner of an expositional minor league baseball team, the Chattanooga Lookouts, and general weirdo known as the P. T. Barnum of baseball, because of the odd stunts he had his players do for publicity. Joe signed her to the Lookouts, because, in the 1930s, recruiting a delicate girl with a wicked changeup was the same sort of novelty as having canaries in the grandstand. (Joe also famously traded a player for a turkey and then ate the turkey. Anything for a headline.)

Jackie signed on the dotted line, becoming the second woman after Lizzy Murphy to play organized baseball in American history.

At the tender age of seventeen, Jackie was enlisted to pitch an exposition game. Her Lookouts were coming up to bat against the big bad pin-striped Yankees. It was another one of Joe Engel's publicity stunts—put his little minor leaguers against the Yankees, then charge by the head to watch them be eviscerated while enjoying peanuts and Cracker Jacks.

At this time, the Yankees' lineup included Babe Ruth and Lou Gehrig, two of the most famous players in baseball history.

The Lookouts? They had Jackie Mitchell.

With a left-handed lady pitcher at the mound, the press leading up to the exposition game was, predictably, sopping with acidic sexism. "The ball won't be the only thing that has curves," one paper wrote, and across America women vibrated with the effort it took not to roll their eyes.

But Jackie was good-natured about it, and on the day of the game, she powdered her nose on the pitcher's mound for a photo op and probably simpered something like, "I am but a simple girl, better with a ball of yarn than a ball of base, what is sports?"

Halfway through the first inning, the Lookouts' starting pitcher was one walk short of a marathon, so their coach subbed Jackie in, just as Babe Ruth stepped up to the plate. He gave Jacks a tip of the hat and assumed a stance known as the "easiest run of my life" crouch.

And then Jackie wound up. Let it fly. And struck that son of a bitch out.

Next, Lou Gehrig sauntered up to the plate and assumed said baseball batting stance (I'm not a sports person). Jackie pulled back like a bow string.

And struck him out, too.

Teen Jackie had just bested the two greatest baseball players in sports history like a baller, a feat that caused the *New York Times* to comment on the exclusion of women from baseball: "The prospect grows gloomier for misogynists."

But apparently none of those misogynists in American sports could handle that. Joe Engel, who set up the game and had apparently not meant for Jackie to strike out two of the majorist players, immediately cancelled her contract. Baseball commissioner Kenesaw Mountain Landis, despite being in possession of the greatest name of all time, supported this choice because, as he said, baseball was "too strenuous" for women. *The Sporting News* suggested Ruth and Gehrig were too gentlemanly to hit the ball against a girl and had struck out on purpose. Babe Ruth, who had sort of cancelled out that speculated gentlemanliness by yelling at the umpire and kicking at the dirt after the strike was called, trashed Jackie in the press, saying, "[Women] will never make good [players]. . . . They are too delicate. It would kill them to play ball every day."

But Jackie kept playing. She needed none of the MLB/MiLB and their sexist garbage! She joined the House of David—a barnstorming team best described as the baseball equivalent of the Harlem Globetrotters, but on elephants. After touring with the House of David, Jackie retired in 1937, at the age of twenty-three, because she was sick of being treated like a sideshow act instead of a legit baseball player just because of her gender. Which makes me weep, because imagine what this lady could have done if her talent had been defined less by the fact that she did not have actual balls than by the fact that she had fast ones.

I feel morally obligated to note that some sports writers have speculated that Babe Ruth and Lou Gehrig struck out on purpose in order for the game to make headlines. It was all for show. There is no evidence for this beyond whining and speculation, so chalk it up to male fragility. Everyone involved maintained it was legit. Including Babe, Lou, and Jackie.

Although the voided contract after the expo game only applied to Jackie, it effectively banned all women from playing baseball professionally. The official banning of women from MiLB and its affiliated leagues appeared in 1952, when the Harrisburg Senators attempted to sign shortstop Eleanor Engle and were blocked.

NOOR INAYAT KHAN

1914–1944, ENGLAND AND FRANCE

The Indian Princess Who Spied for the Allies

Most stories of heroism in Nazi-occupied Europe during World War II don't feature literal royalty, but that's exactly what Noor Inayat Khan was.

Noor was an Indian woman born in Russia and raised in London and Paris, a descendant of Tipu Sultan, the eighteenth-century Muslim ruler of Mysore who had fought British colonialism in India with the help of Napoleon. Her father was a devotee of Sufism, a religious offshoot of Islam that is defined by pacifism and sparse living. Noor was raised in a family of five and took on the role of head-of-household at a young age, when her father died unexpectedly.

When World War II broke out, Noor and her family fled Paris for Bordeaux, then England. There, Noor abandoned her career aspirations (pianist, harpist, child psychologist, and children's book writer, to name a few of her prewar interests) and joined first the Women's Auxiliary Air Force and then the British Special Operations Executive, training to be an undercover wireless operator in the field.

And she was HORRIBLE at it. A trainee of the Johnny English rather than the James Bond variety.

Noor's musical training helped win her points at wireless operations, but she cried and cracked during practice interrogations. She was clumsy and scatterbrained and often misplaced her codebooks. She was freaked out by weapons. Not to mention she was a pacifist (though that pacifism bred in her the intense hatred toward the Nazis that led her to joining up in the first place), pretty meh about patriotism (because of the aforementioned familial legacy of ill-will toward the British colonization of India, though she did hope that any heroic efforts on her part could help bridge the gap between the English and the Indians), and, as an Indian Muslim woman, she didn't blend in well in 1940s France. Training reports described her as "not overburdened with brains" and "unsuited for work," which is a really unnecessarily savage performance evaluation.

So no one expected much of Noor.

But England was kind of desperate, and Noor was kind of there.

So they dropped her into Paris with only a French ration card, a lethal pill in case she was captured, and a false identity. She was assigned to work in the Prosper network as an undercover wireless operator, one of the most dangerous jobs for an agent in the field. Using radio direction-finding equipment put wireless operators in unique danger, since it allowed the Security Service of the Reichsführer-SS to pinpoint their location, but it was vital work for conveying information back to the British forces in England. Most wireless operators were captured after just a few weeks in France.

Less than a week after she arrived, her entire network was captured, leaving Noor one of the only British wireless operators in Paris. Which was panic-inducing on the part of the SOE. Their only connection to the French resistance was a clumsy pacifist with emotional issues.

But when the British sent word to Noor that she should lie low, she telegrammed back (I'm paraphrasing, but I think the spirit is the same), "Don't worry—I'm gonna freaking crush this."

And then she freaking crushed it.

Code named "Madeleine," Noor outsmarted, outmaneuvered, and sometimes literally outran the Nazis. She changed identities almost daily. All the while, she sent information back to Britain in twenty minute bursts (as long of a transmission as she could risk), doing the work of nearly six agents all on her own. For a time, she was the only link between England and the French resistance. Once, when caught by a Nazi soldier while stringing up her radio wire, she sweet-talked him not only into letting her go but helping her get that radio wire up where she could get a signal.

When England told her she had done enough and could come home proud, she refused. There was more work to do.

Noor survived five months on the ground in France when the average life of an undercover agent in Paris was six weeks. When the Nazis finally caught her, she did not go gently into that good night. We're talking kicking, screaming, and multiple escape attempts (one that included an honest-to-God bedsheet rope). Noor spent ten months in a German prison, mostly chained in solitary since she was considered "very dangerous." She never cracked, even under brutal interrogation. She gave the Nazis nothing.

Noor was executed in the Dachau concentration camp after almost a year of brutal imprisonment.

Her last word, according to the other prisoners, was *Liberté.*

For her heroism, Noor was posthumously awarded the George Cross in 1949 and the Croix de guerre.

FANNY BLANKERS-KOEN

1918–2004, THE NETHERLANDS

The Fastest Woman in the World

The highlight of Fanny Blankers-Koen's first Olympic Games was getting the autograph of her all-time number one favorite athlete, Jesse Owens. Even though she didn't medal or place in the track and field events she competed in, she got to meet her hero and totally fangirl over him.

Years later, when she met him again and introduced herself, it was Jess Owens's turn to fangirl. According to Fanny, he said, "You don't have to tell me who you are, I know everything about you."

What happened between that first, uneventful Olympics in 1936 and that second meeting with Jesse Owens?

At the 1936 Olympics, Fanny competed in the high jump and the 4 x 100-meter relay but missed out on a spot on the podium in both. But she wasn't worried—she was only eighteen, and when the Olympics rolled around again, she'd still be young enough to compete.

But then World War II happened. The Olympics were cancelled in 1940, a week before Fanny's home country of the Netherlands was invaded.

Over the course of World War II, Fanny married Jan Blankers, a sports journalist whose attitude had been that women shouldn't compete in athletics, until he fell hard for Fanny and saw what a dummy he'd been. During the war, Fanny continued to run and train, though nutrition was tough because food was scarce. When she gave birth to their first child in 1941, the Dutch sports press assumed her athletic career was over.

When the first postwar Olympics rolled around, Fanny was thirty years old and dismissed by many as being too old and too much of a mom to compete. She had two children, and she later told the *New York Times* about the hateful letters she received telling her she should be ashamed for training and competing in track and field when she should be staying home with her children (and also for daring to wear shorts—no self-respecting mother should let the world see her legs!).

But Fanny qualified to compete in the 100-meter, the 200-meter, and 80-meter hurdles and the 4 x 100-meter relay at the 1948 Summer Olympics in London, the first games since World War II.

She received gold medals in all four.

At the Olympics, Fanny ran in the pouring rain, won the hurdles by a photo finish, completed the 200-meter 7/10 of a second before the silver medalist—the largest margin of victory in any Olympic 200-meter final. She was the last runner on her relay team and brought them back from a poor start that seemed certain to result in a last-place finish. She was the first woman to win four Olympic gold medals. That's still the most medals a female track-and-field athlete has won in a single Olympics. With each victory, Fanny demolished prejudices about gender, age, and motherhood and helped establish the legitimacy of women in sports. Female athletes around the world still venerate her.

Fanny was dubbed "The Flying Housewife" (also "The Flying Dutchmam" and "Amazing Fanny"). She was welcomed home to Amsterdam by an immense crowd and with many presents—including a bicycle given to her by the city itself, so she "need not run so much." Queen Juliana of the Netherlands made her a Knight of the Order of Orange-Nassau, a chivalry order for "everyone who has earned special merits for society."

"ALL I'VE DONE IS RUN FAST. I DON'T SEE WHY PEOPLE SHOULD MAKE MUCH FUSS ABOUT THAT."

Throughout her athletics career, she set numerous world records and won medals and awards beyond the Olympics. After she retired, she served as a team leader for the Dutch Athletics Team. In honor of her achievements, the Fanny Blankers-Koen Games were established in 1981 and are still held annually in the Netherlands.

In 1999, Fanny was declared "Female Athlete of the Century" by the International Association of Athletics Federations. No one was surprised by this—except Fanny. Upon the announcement, she said with audible shock, "You mean it's me who has won?"

KUMANDER LIWAYWAY

1919–2014, PHILIPPINES

The Woman Who Wore Lipstick into Battle

Every warrior needs a signature fighting style.

And for Kumander Liwayway, that signature was getting her hair done, buffing her nails, and meticulously applying red lipstick before each battle she led in the Huk Revolution.

Which brings a whole new meaning to fighting like a girl.

Born Remedios Gomez-Paraiso, she grew up in the Philippines, where her father was a mayor. Remedios was basically a Disney Channel teenager. She loved dancing, pretty clothes, perfumes, and dressmaking, was a local beauty queen, and was voted "least likely to wield machine guns against invading forces" in her high school yearbook.

And then the Huk Rebellion happened.

What is the Huk Rebellion?

Lemme tell ya.

The Huk Rebellion, which began during World War II, is shorthand for Hukbalahap Rebellion, named for the Tagalog acronym for Hukbo ng Bayan Laban sa Hapon, which translates to "People's Anti-Japanese Army," so no one was being subtle about who they disliked.

When the Japanese invaded Remedios's town, her father tried to organize a branch of this people's army, but he was discovered by the Japanese overlords before he could make any real movement. For his insubordination, he was tortured and killed, and his body was displayed in the town.

Which is when Remedios became less a teenage Disney Channel beauty queen and more a Tarantino badass.

With no military training and not even a high school diploma, twenty-two-year-old Remedios joined a group of guerrilla rebels fighting against Japan. She took the name Kumander Liwayway—"Commander Dawn," the sort of moniker that begs to be slapped on the front of a comic book. Kumander Liwayway's first military job was with the medical team, but she was quickly promoted to squadron commander once it became clear that she had the sort of fighting spirit that would make her the star of the nightmares of any man who dared cross her. Soon, Kumander Liwayway was overseeing nearly two hundred soldiers and leading them on dangerous missions to rescue downed American pilots and steal guns and supplies from their Japanese adversaries.

Liwayway became famous among the Huk rebels after her squad fought the Japanese at the Battle of Kamansi. They were getting their asses handed to them, so their commanding officer called for retreat in the face of Japanese forces, Liwayway told her men to hold positions and keep up the good fight. When Filipino reinforcements arrived, they found Liwayway and her soldiers still slugging it out with the enemy and definitely not in need of rescuing.

"ONE OF THE THINGS I AM FIGHTING FOR IN THIS MOVEMENT IS THE RIGHT TO BE MYSELF."

With her styled hair and red lipstick (which she adopted before every battle, both to appear calm so her men would similarly feel at ease before battle, and also because she just liked looking fabulous) and a predilection for fighting men who made sexually aggressive comments

toward her, she may not have been the most traditional military leader among the Huk Rebels. But she was certainly an effective one.

Liwayway was captured twice. The first time, she gave some ovation-worthy sass to the president of the Philippines' face when he called her a terrorist—"Who are the Huks, Mr. President? Ninety-five percent are families of peasants, so I cannot see any reason why the Huks will terrorize their own families or why the parents will be afraid of their own children." The second time, her husband was killed and she was thrown in solitary confinement. When she was put on trial, she claimed that she was innocent because, as a simple woman, she was just supporting her husband in the fight and couldn't be held responsible for her actions. Which is one of the first times in history sexism has worked in a woman's favor, because the argument worked and she was acquitted.

After her second imprisonment, Liwayway didn't go back to the war but instead became an advocate for soldiers who had returned home. As part of the Huks Veteran Organization, Liwayway lobbied for pensions for soldiers for more than twenty years, continuing in her tradition of leaving no man behind.

About 10 percent of soldiers in the Huk Rebellion were women. They worked as spies, nurses, soldiers, couriers, and military leaders. It was the first time women had been integrated into Filipino military forces, and they dealt with a lot of sexism and discrimination from their male counterparts, who considered them to just be following their men around.

AZUCENA VILLAFLOR

1924–1977, ARGENTINA

Marching for Argentina's Disappeared

Hell hath no fury like a mom on a mission.

And Azucena Villaflor was mom to all of Argentina.

Born outside Buenos Aires to a working-class family involved in the Peronist movement, Azucena had a grade school education, four children and a husband, and a minimum-wage job as a telephone operator. A pretty average life.

Around the time Azucena and her husband became empty nesters, Argentina was in a state of political upheaval known as the "Dirty War," which lasted from 1976 to 1983. During that time, the military government abducted, tortured, and killed anyone considered subversive, from left-wing militants to all political opponents of the regime, many of whom were very young. The kidnapped people were referred to as the "disappeared," but everyone knew what had happened to them—they were murdered. The government obliterated any records that would help the families find the bodies or even know for sure what had happened to their children.

Nestor, Azucena's son, was one of these young rebels who had abandoned studying architecture in order to organize political dissent and help those stepped on by the military regime. As a result of his subversions, Nestor and his partner, Raquel Mangin, were arrested and disappeared.

Most people accepted that their disappeared family members and loved ones were lost to them and understood that poking around would only get them in trouble, too. But Azucena poked anyway. She made inquiries at the Interior Ministry after her son and, though she didn't get past the secretaries, she asked questions. And asked. And asked.

And when she didn't get answers, she organized.

Since no one had been able to get results at the ground level, Azucena decided to go straight to the top: She organized a protest of mothers of disappeared children outside the government offices of General Jorge Rafael Videla, the leader of Argentina's military junta.

Led by Azucena, mothers met in cafés, churches, and living rooms around Buenos Aires to organize. They first appeared publicly in the Plaza de Mayo on the afternoon of April 30, 1977. Only about twenty women were there, but they decided to continue meeting on the plaza every Thursday until they got results. The group's only rule was that only mothers could join. Most of them were housewives, and many had never worked outside their home, let alone been political dissidents. The symbol of the protests became the white headscarves the mothers wore when they marched, sometimes with the names of their disappeared children written on them.

And slowly, the mothers became a movement.

The small protest group of women became a horde that marched the plaza every Thursday afternoon and drove the Argentinean government crazy. Their message soon expanded as the media covered their protests and awareness of the disappeared began to spread around the world. In an attempt to silence public unrest, the government placed a ban on people stopping or gathering in the square, but the mothers cleverly circumnavigated that law by walking around it instead. And at the center of it all was Azucena, who always carried a folder with information about her missing son and rallied the women with the phrase, "Todas por todas y todos son nuestros hijos" (All, for all are our children).

On December 10, 1977, the mothers published a list of the names of all their missing children and distributed it around Buenos Aires. That same night, Azucena was abducted, taken to a notorious Argentinean torture center, and then flung from a plane into the ocean on a "death flight." A few months later, her body washed up on the beach.

The military regime in Argentina fell in 1983, and democracy was restored, but the mothers remain a major force in political reform to this day. Every Thursday they still march around the Plaza in their white headscarves and continue to fight for human, political, and civil rights for Latin Americans and people all over the world.

"TODAS POR TODAS Y TODOS SON NUESTROS HIJOS / ALL, FOR ALL ARE OUR CHILDREN."

A government commission has put the number of unresolved disappearances in Argentina during this time at about 11,000; the mothers claim it's closer to 30,000.

ANGELA MORLEY

1924–2009, ENGLAND

Composer, Conductor, Transgender Pioneer

You'd be hard-pressed to find a human who can't hum the opening lines of Darth Vader's theme, "The Imperial March," or describe one of the iconic scenes it underscores in *Star Wars: The Empire Strikes Back.*

It would be far more difficult to find someone who knows that John Williams's longtime collaborator on that film and many others was Angela Morley, a transgender woman who is responsible for some of the most memorable scores in film and television.

Angela was born Walter Stott, and her father was a watchmaker who played a ukulele on the side, so she grew up in a home of rhythm and melody. In high school, she began playing the piano, violin, accordion, clarinet, and alto sax and became such a proficient musician she was able to drop out of school to go on the road with a swing band made up entirely of teens. She played for the equivalent of two dollars a week.

Angela might have been one of the few Britons who can say they had good things come out of World War II. Musicians around the country were being drafted, but since Angela was too young to be recruited and also a hell of a sight reader, she was quickly able to work her way up to bandleader.

After a decade of touring, Angela quit life on the road to take up composing, which she had been studying on the side. She was appointed head of the British branch of Philips Records before going on to conduct and write cues for two long-running radio shows and later began scoring films for Associated British Picture Corporation.

And, most importantly, she wrote Britain's entries for the Eurovision Song Contest.

In 1972, Angela vanished from the music business, only to return a few years later fully transitioned and writing, composing, and living as a woman under her new name. The 1970s London music scene didn't exactly welcome her with open arms—it was more of a hypermasculine boys club than a Pride parade. Angela had to endure discrimination, snide comments, and general small-mindedness due to her decision to transition.

But Angela didn't have time for cisgender nonsense. She had film scores to compose, like the soundtrack to the animated adaptation of *Watership Down*, a project she took on when the original composer dropped out three days before recording was scheduled to begin. She composed the entire score in two weeks. One success led to another, and in 1974, she was nominated for an Academy Award for her work on *The Little Prince*, then again in 1976 for *The Slipper and the Rose*.

Hollywood, as it turns out, was far kinder to a British transwoman than London, so after having the time of her life at both Oscars ceremonies, Angela picked up and moved to Beverly Hills. There, she focused mainly on songwriting for television, and her credits include *Dallas*, *Dynasty*, *Cagney & Lacey*, and *Wonder Woman*. In Hollywood, she also struck up a friendship with composer John Williams, and after probably getting little half-heart "best friends forever" pendants, she became his uncredited collaborator and frequent orchestrator on blockbusters like *Star Wars*, *The Empire Strikes Back*, *ET*, *Home Alone*, and *Schindler's List*. She also

contributed to soundtracks for *Hook*, *The Karate Kid*, and *Superman* (and Disney's *The Hunchback of Notre Dame II*, but we won't hold that straight-to-VHS monstrosity against her).

After retiring from the movie business, Angela worked as orchestrator, arranger, and sometimes conductor with musicians such as Yo-Yo Ma, Julie Andrews, Itzhak Perlman, and Benny Goodman, as well as for orchestras and symphonies around the world. She won three Emmy Awards and was nominated eleven times before her death in 2009 at the age of eighty-four.

"DO YOU KNOW THE SCENE IN STAR WARS WHERE LUKE GOES DOWN INTO THE DEATH STAR TRENCH AND THE VOICE SAYS 'USE THE FORCE, LUKE'? THAT'S MY ORCHESTRATION."

MARIA TALLCHIEF

1925–2013, UNITED STATES

America's First Prima Ballerina

In the twentieth-century ballet scene, the only way to make it big was to have a Russian surname. The Russians were the universally acknowledged lords of the dance world, so the best way to get picked out of the chorus line as a ballerina was to have a Russian name on your resume. And since most dancers didn't, a lot lied.

Maria Tallchief was definitely not a Russian-sounding name. But despite suggestions from teachers and colleagues that she could morph into the drastically more Soviet *Tallchieva* without a lot of fuss, which would probably result in more jobs and less racism, Maria refused.

If she was going to be the first prima ballerina in the United States, she was going to do it under her own American-Indian name.

Born Elizabeth Marie Tallchief on an Oklahoma reservation, Maria's talent for dance was apparent from a young age. At three, she started lessons, and by age eight, her whole family had moved to Los Angeles to get better dancing lessons for both her and her younger sister. At age seventeen, Maria joined the prestigious Ballet Russe de Monte Carlo. It was there she met choreographer George Balanchine and became his muse and later his wife. When Balanchine cofounded what would become the New York City Ballet in 1948, Maria became the company's first star.

> **"A CREATURE OF MAGIC, DANCING THE SEEMINGLY IMPOSSIBLE WITH EFFORTLESS BEAUTY OF MOVEMENT, ELECTRIFYING US WITH HER BRILLIANCE, ENCHANTING US WITH HER RADIANCE OF BEING."**
> **Walter Terry**

George's complicated, intricate choreography and Maria's on point execution of it, combined with her signature passion and energy, revolutionized ballet in the United States and set a high standard for other dancers that followed her in the roles she originated. Performing George's choreography required athleticism, speed, technique, and aggression, an unreasonable combination that made it impossible for many dancers. Maria was one of the few who could not just dance it but dance it *flawlessly*. Dance critic John Martin of the *New York Times* wrote that her role in *The Firebird*, choreography that George created for her, required her "to do everything except spin on her head, and she does it with complete and incomparable brilliance."

The Firebird jumpstarted the New York City Ballet's success, and it helped define Maria's place as America's first prima ballerina. She went on to originate dozens of iconic roles and revolutionize ballet with her immaculate execution of George's innovative and grueling choreography. Her roles in George Balanchine originals included the title role in *Swan Lake*, as well as the Sugarplum Fairy in *The Nutcracker*, a performance that helped bring the ballet out of obscurity and transform it into America's favorite holiday tradition. In addition to her work with the New York City Ballet, she became the first American to dance with the Paris Opera Ballet and played Anna Pavlova across from Esther Williams in the film *Million Dollar Mermaid*.

After leaving the New York City Ballet, Maria traveled the world, racking up honors, including induction into the National Women's Hall of Fame and a Kennedy Center Honor. She became the first American to perform in the legendary Bolshoi Theater in Moscow. When she returned to the Ballet Russe de Monte Carlo in 1954, she was the highest paid dancer in the United States.

She died in 2013, at age eighty-eight.

THE MIRABAL SISTERS

1930s – 1960, DOMINICAN REPUBLIC

The Sisters Who Toppled a Dictatorship

In the 1930s, the Dominican Republic was ruled by dictator Rafael Trujillo, who was terrible. Under Trujillo, basic human rights were nonexistent. He massacred thousands, led genocide against Haitians, and his enemies had a way of disappearing mysteriously. He owned and controlled most of the utilities in the country, and he used them to further both his dictatorial nonsense and his own financial gains. He employed spies around the country to let him know who was speaking against him, and he sent scouts to find women for him to rape.

And it's in the face of that horrific rule that four sisters—Patria, Dedé, Minerva, and María Teresa Mirabal—stood up and refused to normalize tyranny any longer.

Despite growing up in the aggressively housewifey 1940s, three of the four sisters went to college (and the one who didn't, Dedé, helped run the family business). Minerva got involved in anti-Trujillo clubs while in law school, but her revolutionary involvement came to a head when she met Trujillo at a party, where he attempted to get his hands up her skirt. And Minerva shut. Him. Down. By slapping him across the face.

Trujillo threw a mantrum because Minerva refused his sexual advances, so, in retaliation, he did everything he could to ruin her career. In her second year of law school, she was barred from classrooms unless she spoke out in support of Trujillo (spoiler alert: she didn't), and when she finally graduated, the government mysteriously denied her a license to practice law without giving a reason.

And it didn't stop there. The Mirabal sisters' father was imprisoned and tortured for apparently no reason, though it seemed pretty related to Minerva rejecting Trujillo. The imprisonment resulted in their father's death shortly thereafter. Around the same time, Minerva and their mother were held as hostages by Trujillo's goons in a hotel on a trip to Santo Domingo. Minerva was told they would be released only if she slept with Trujillo (don't worry, they escaped).

Which is when Minerva had just about had enough and decided something had to be done about this dictator. And she and her sisters were the ones to do it.

Her sisters María Teresa and Patria were quick to join her anti-Trujillo cause. While Patria was on a religious retreat (she wanted to be a nun), she had witnessed a massacre of civilians by Trujillo's men, so the sisters started a revolutionary movement called the 14th of June Movement (the date of the massacre). Their mission statement was "hell-bent on toppling a tyrant." As their supporters grew, the sisters did everything they could to raise awareness of the truth behind the government's abuse of power, bring Trujillo down, and restore democracy to the Dominican Republic. They distributed pamphlets about people Trujillo had killed and tracked down the truth about those who had been disappeared. They built guns and bombs. They spoke out against Trujillo's abuse of human rights and his regime's brutality.

In short, they resisted.

"WE CANNOT ALLOW OUR CHILDREN TO GROW UP IN THIS CORRUPT AND TYRANNICAL REGIME. WE HAVE TO FIGHT AGAINST IT, AND I AM WILLING TO GIVE UP EVERYTHING, EVEN MY LIFE IF NECESSARY."

Patria Mirabal

Their code name among the movement was Las Mariposas (the Butterflies).

The sisters endured torture and abuse for their efforts. Minerva and María Teresa were arrested and tortured multiple times, as were their husbands. Their property was seized. Their family separated. But Minerva, Patria, and María Teresa refused to give up.

They did not live to see the glory of their fight. On November 25, 1960 María Teresa, Minerva, and Patria were assassinated by Trujillo's men on their way home from visiting their husbands in prison. Their deaths were covered up with a lie about a car accident.

The sisters' deaths outraged the Dominican Republic. Their revolutionary efforts and martyrdom helped spark the campaign that led to Trujillo's assassination six months later.

The legacy of the Mirabal sisters lives on into modern day. You can find them on the 200-pesos bill in the Dominican Republic. The United Nations designated November 25 as the International Day for the Elimination of Violence against Women in their memory. And an obelisk built by Trujillo when he renamed Santo Domingo after himself is covered in murals of the sisters. Which is some vigilante justice.

The fourth sister, Dedé, was way less involved in the actual government overthrow than her sisters (and also, she was not assassinated), but she was still a badass in her own right. She spent her life running the family business, caring for her sisters' children after their deaths, and preserving the legacy of the Butterflies. You can still visit a museum dedicated to them in the Dominican Republic that was founded by Dedé. She died in 2014, after a life dedicated to making sure the world remembered her sisters and their sacrifice.

LORRAINE HANSBERRY

1930–1965, UNITED STATES

Playwright for Civil Rights

Lorraine Hansberry grew up on familiar terms with how tough it was to be a black woman in America.

She was the granddaughter of a former slave. As a child, her family was brutally attacked when they moved into an all-white neighborhood. When they refused to leave their home, the resulting court case was taken all the way up to the Supreme Court. When she was fifteen, her father died, and Lorraine swore that part of what killed him was the toll of American racism.

It was these early injustices that inspired Lorraine's activism. In college at the University of Wisconsin–Madison, she fought for integrated dormitories, and, after two years of higher education, she moved to Harlem to pursue the kind of education you can only get from standing on picket lines for civil rights. She helped move the furniture of evicted tenants back into their homes, studied African history under W. E. B. Du Bois, and wrote for the Pan-African monthly *Freedom*.

It was on one of those picket lines that she met Robert Nemiroff, a white Jewish boy, composer, future Broadway producer, and clearly a kindred spirit, because the night before their wedding, they skipped their rehearsal dinner to protest the execution of the Rosenbergs.

Despite their shared interest in justice and the fact that their marriage wasn't terrible, it was still doomed from the start because Lorraine was a lesbian. Aside from adding LGBTQ rights to the list of causes she picketed for, Lorraine was a subscriber to *The Ladder*, the first subscription-based lesbian magazine in the United States, which had to be delivered in brown paper bags to avoid notice by the postmen. Her letters to *The Ladder* reveal her own struggles with her sexuality and her experience as a closeted lesbian in a heterosexual relationship.

Lorraine knew how to hustle for her dreams. She worked as a cashier and a waitress while writing at night until her husband wrote a hit song, allowing her to write full time. During this time, she wrote *The Crystal Stair*, named for a line from a Langston Hughes poem. The play was about a struggling black family in Chicago. Lorraine later renamed it

A Raisin in the Sun, a different line from a different Langston Hughes poem.

You might have heard of this play. It's what you might call *prolific*.

(More on the subject of her not-terrible marriage: Despite her queerness, Lorraine credited Robert as being the one to fish pages of *A Raisin in the Sun* out of the garbage when she threw them out in a fit of frustrated writer rage, and even after their separation, they continued to work together.)

"NEVER BEFORE IN THE ENTIRE HISTORY OF THE AMERICAN THEATRE HAD SO MUCH OF THE TRUTH OF BLACK PEOPLE'S LIVES BEEN SEEN ON THE STAGE."

James Baldwin

On March 11, 1959, *A Raisin in the Sun* opened on Broadway, the first play written by an African American woman to be produced on the Great White Way. Later that year, Lorraine became the first black playwright and the youngest American to win a New York Drama Critics' Circle award. The show ran for 530 performances over fifteen months.

Her only other produced play during her lifetime, *The Sign in Sidney Brustein's Window*, was met with meh reviews and closed on January 12, 1965, around the time Lorraine died, a life cut tragically short by pancreatic cancer. At her funeral, she was eulogized by James Baldwin and Martin Luther King, Jr. Her ex-husband continued to produce and publish her works posthumously, including a collection of her writing adapted into a stage play called *To Be Young, Gifted and Black*, which was later published as a memoir and inspired a Nina Simone song.

BIBLIOGRAPHY

Abbott, Karen. "The Life and Crimes of 'Old Mother' Mandelbuam." *Smithsonian Magazine*, September 6, 2011. http://www.smithsonianmag.com/history/the-life-and-crimes-of-old-mother-mandelbaum-71693582/.

Abdullahi, Mohamed Diriye. *Culture and Customs of Somalia*. Westport, Connecticut: Greenwood Press, 2001.

Agonito, Rosemary, and Joseph Agonito. "Resurrecting History's Forgotten Women: A Case Study from the Cheyenne Indians." *Frontiers: A Journal of Women Studies* no. 3 (Autumn 1981): 8–16. doi: 10.2307/3346202.

Agrawal, Lion M. G. *Freedom Fighters of India*. Delhi: Isha Books, 2008.

Alvarez, Julie. *In the Time of the Butterflies*. Chapel Hill: Algonquin Books, 1994.

American Society of Civil Engineers. "Emily Warren Roebling." http://www.asce.org/templates/person-bio-detail.aspx?id=11203.

Anderson, Jack. "Maria Tallchief, a Dazzling Ballerina and Muse for Balanchine, Dies at 88." *New York Times*, April 12, 2013. http://www.nytimes.com/2013/04/13/arts/dance/maria-tallchief-brilliant-ballerina-dies-at-88.html.

Anderson, Melissa. "Lorraine Hansberry's Letters Reveal the Playwright's Private Struggle." *Village Voice*, February 26, 2014. http://www.villagevoice.com/arts/lorraine-hansberrys-letters-reveal-the-playwrights-private-struggle-7187630.

Anderson, Susan Heller. "Ursula Nordstrom, 78, a Nurturer of Authors for Children, Is Dead." *New York Times*, October 12, 1988. http://www.nytimes.com/1988/10/12/obituaries/ursula-nordstrom-78-a-nurturer-of-authors-for-children-is-dead.html.

Angela Morley. http://www.angelamorley.com/.

"Angela Morley." *Telegraph*, January 25, 2009. http://www.telegraph.co.uk/news/obituaries/4339863/Angela-Morley.html.

Angier, Natalie. "The Mighty Mathematician You've Never Heard Of." *New York Times*, March 26, 2012. http://www.nytimes.com/2012/03/27/science/emmy-noether-the-most-significant-mathematician-youve-never-heard-of.html.

Anne Lister Online. "About Annie Lister." http://www.annelister.co.uk/.

Badass of the Week. "Mochizuki Chiyome." Last modified January 23, 2015. http://www.badassoftheweek.com/index.cgi?id=33837513055.

Bagchi, Rob. "50 stunning Olympic moments No10: Fanny Blankers-Koen wins four golds." *Guardian*, January 18, 2012. https://www.theguardian.com/sport/blog/2012/jan/18/fanny-blankers-koen-olympic-moments.

Banerji, Urvija. "The Chinese Female Pirate Who Commanded 80,000 Outlaws." *Atlas Obscura*, April 6, 2016. http://www.atlasobscura.com/articles/the-chinese-female-pirate-who-commanded-80000-outlaws.

Basu, Shrabani. *Spy Princess: The Life of Noor Inayat Khan*. Omega Publications, 2007.

Bernard, Chelsea. "Murasaki Shikibu: Badass Women in Japanese History." *Tofugu*, August 26, 2014. https://www.tofugu.com/japan/murasaki-shikibu/.

Bharathanatyam. "Smt Rukmini Devi Arundale." http://bharathanatyam.in/about-bharathanatyam/famous-dancers/smt-rukmini-devi-arundale.

Bijkerk, Tom. "Fanny Blankers-Koen: A Biography." *Journal of Olympic History* 12 (May 2004): 56–60.

Biography. "Clelia Duel Mosher." Last modified September 25, 2015. http://www.biography.com/people/clelia-duel-mosher.

BlackPast. "Aba Women's Riots (November–December 1929)." http://www.blackpast.org/gah/aba-womens-riots-november-december-1929.

BlackPast. "Ball, Alice Augusta (1892–1916)." http://www.blackpast.org/aaw/ball-alice-augusta-1892-1916.

Blashfield, Jean F. *Women Inventors, Volume 4*. Minneapolis: Capstone Press, 1996.

Blewett, Kelly. "Ursula Nordstrom and the Queer History of Children's Books." *Los Angeles Review of Books*, August 28, 2016. https://lareviewofbooks.org/article/ursula-nordstrom-and-the-queer-history-of-the-childrens-book/.

Brown, Chip. "The King Herself." *National Geographic*, April 2009. http://ngm.nationalgeographic.com/2009/04/hatshepsut/brown-text.

Brown, Jeannette. *African American Women Chemists*. New York: Oxford University Press, 2011.

Buckley, Veronica. *Christina, Queen of Sweden: The Restless Life of a European Eccentric*. New York: HarperCollins, 2004.

Bundles, A'Lelia. *On Her Own Ground: The Life and Times of Madam CJ Walker*. New York: Simon and Schuster, 2001.

Cavendish, Margaret. *The Blazing World*. Originally printed in London: A. Mazwell, 1668.

Cavendish, Richard. "The Abdication of Queen Christina of Sweden." *History Today* 54, no.6 (2004). http://www.historytoday.com/richard-cavendish/abdication-queen-christina-sweden.

Cavna, Michael. "Emmy Noether Google Doodle: Why Einstein Called Her a 'Creative Mathematical Genius.'" *Washington Post*, March 23, 2015. https://www.washingtonpost.com/news/comic-riffs/wp/2015/03/23/emmy-noether-google-doodle-why-einstein-called-her-a-creative-mathematical-genius/?utm_term=.179c4305b0ef.

Chauhan, Subhadra Kumari. "Jhansi Ki Rani (With English Translation)." *All Poetry.* https://allpoetry.com/Jhansi-Ki-Rani-(With-English-Translation.

Cheng, Selina. "The Oldest Library on Earth Was Started by a Woman, and Finally Everyone Can Visit It." *Quartz,* July 3, 2016. https://qz.com/708139/the-worlds-oldest-university-and-library-in-morocco-founded-and-restored-by-two-women/.

Chicago Public Library. "Lorraine Hansberry Biography." https://www.chipublib.org/lorraine-hansberry-biography/.

Code Name: Butterflies. "The Story." http://www.codenamebutterflies.org/story.html.

Colonial Zone. "Museo Hermanas Mirabal/Mirabal Sisters Museum." http://www.colonialzone-dr.com/mirabal-museum.html.

Conway, J. North. "Meet 'The Queen of Thieves' Marm Mandelbaum, New York City's First Crime Boss." *Daily Beast,* September 7, 2014. https://www.thedailybeast.com/meet-the-queen-of-thieves-marm-mandelbaum-new-york-citys-first-mob-boss

Conway, J. North. *Queen of Thieves: The True Story of "Marm" Mandelbaum and Her Gangs of New York.* New York: Skyhorse Publishing, 2014.

Cook, Bernard A. *Women and War.* Santa Barbara: ABC-CLIO, 2006.

Cordery, Stacy A. *Juliette Gordon Low: The Remarkable Founder of the Girl Scouts.* New York: Viking, 2012.

Crampton, Caroline. "The Lesbian Dead Sea Scrolls: Annie Lister's Diaries." *NewStatesman,* December 5, 2013. http://www.newstatesman.com/culture/2013/11/lesbian-dead-sea-scrolls.

Crawford, Elizabeth. *The Womens' Suffrage Movement.* London: Routledge, 2001.

Dalton, Samantha. "Noor Inayat Khan: The Indian Princess Who Spied for Britain, BBC News." BBC News, November 8, 2012. http://www.bbc.com/news/uk-20240693.

de Orsúa y Vela, Bartolomé Arzáns. *Stories of the Imperial Town of Potosí.* Providence: Brown University Press, 1965.

Dillon, Richard H. *North American Indian Wars.* Facts on File, 1983.

Directors Guild of America. "Dorothy Arzner." http://www.dga.org/Craft/DGAQ/All-Articles/0604-Winter2006-07/Legends-Dorothy-Arzner.aspx.

Doster, Adam. "The Myth of Jackie Mitchell, the Girl Who Struck Out Ruth and Gehrig." *The Daily Beast,* May 13, 2013. http://www.thedailybeast.com/articles/2013/05/18/the-myth-of-jackie-mitchell-the-girl-who-struck-out-ruth-and-gehrig.html.

Duncombe, Laura Sook. "Sayyida al-Hurra, the Beloved, Avenging Islamic Pirate Queen." *Pictorial,* March 3, 2015. http://pictorial.jezebel.com/sayyida-al-hurra-the-beloved-avenging-islamic-pirate-1685524517.

Encyclopedia.com. "Murasaki Shikibu." http://www.encyclopedia.com/people/literature-and-arts/asian-literature-biographies/murasaki-shikibu.

Encyclopedia Britannica. "Crimean War." Last modified March 7, 2017. https://www.britannica.com/event/Crimean-War.

Encyclopedia Britannica. "Hukbalahap Rebellion." https://www.britannica.com/event/Hukbalahap-Rebellion.

Encyclopedia Britannica. "Lakshmi Bai." Last modified January 25, 2016. https://www.britannica.com/biography/Lakshmi-Bai.

Encyclopedia Britannica. "Sybil Ludington." Last modified May 18, 2016. https://www.britannica.com/biography/Sybil-Ludington.

Encyclopedia Britannica. "Trung Sisters." Last modified, March 1, 2016. https://www.britannica.com/topic/Trung-Sisters.

Encyclopedia of Fashion. "Silk." http://www.fashionencyclopedia.com/fashion_costume_culture/Early-Cultures-Asia/Silk.html.

Enemy of the Reich. "A Muslim Woman Defies the Nazis in WW II Paris." http://www.enemyofthereich.com/.

Everett, George. "Mary Fields, Female Pioneer in Montana." *HistoryNet,* June 12, 2006. http://www.historynet.com/mary-fields-female-pioneer-in-montana.htm.

Farmer, Fannie. *The Fannie Farmer Cookbook.* Originally published in New York: Random House, 1896.

FBK Games. http://www.fbkgames.nl/

Feeding America: The Historic American Cookbook Project. "Farmer, Fannie Merritt." http://digital.lib.msu.edu/projects/cookbooks/html/authors/author_farmer.cfm.

Gandhi, Gopalkrishna. "The Woman Who Said No: How Rukmini Devi Chose Dance Over Presidency" *Hindu Times,* March 4, 2016. http://www.hindustantimes.com/columns/the-woman-who-said-no-how-rukmini-devi-chose-dance-over-presidency/story-5OKAXlRoN46d8QfiUX1QWI.html.

Gardiner, Kelly. *Goddess.* Australia: HarperCollins. 2014.

Gardner, Isabella Stewart, and Hilliard T. Goldfarb. *The Isabella Stewart Gardner Museum: A Companion Guide and History.* New Haven: Yale University Press, 1995.

Gariwo. "Exemplary Figures Reported by Gariwo: Azucena Villaflor 1924–1977: Founder of the Mothers of Plaza de Mayo." http://en.gariwo.net/righteous/the-righteous-biographies/civil-courage/exemplary-figures-reported-by-gariwo/azucena-villaflor-7615.html.

Gates, Henry Louis, Jr. "Madam Walker, the First Black American Woman to Be a Self-Made Millionaire." PBS. http://www.pbs.org/wnet/african-americans-many-rivers-to-cross/history/100-amazing-facts/madam-walker-the-first-black-american-woman-to-be-a-self-made-millionaire/.

Gaughan, Gavin. "Angela Morley." *Guardian,* January 22, 2009. https://www.theguardian.com/culture/2009/jan/23/angela-morley-obituary-wally-stott.

Gautier, Theophile. *Mademoiselle de Maupin.* Originally printed in London: Gibbings & Company, Limited, 1899.

Geiling, Natasha. "The Women Who Mapped the Universe and Still Couldn't Get Any Respect." *Smithsonian Magazine,* September 18, 2013. http://www.smithsonianmag.com/history/the-women-who-mapped-the-universe-and-still-couldnt-get-any-respect-9287444/.

Girl Scouts Official Website. http://www.girlscouts.org/.

Godfrey, Emelyne. *Femininity, Crime and Self-Defence in Victorian Literature and Society.* London: Palgrave Macmillan, 2012.

Grundhauser, Eric. *New York's First Female Crime Boss Started Her Own Crime School*. Atlas Obscura, March 23, 2016. http://www.atlasobscura.com/articles/new-yorks-first-female-crime-boss-started-her-own-crime-school.

Gupta, Indra. *India's 50 Most Illustrious Women*. Icon Publications, 2003.

Halzack, Sarah. "Maria Tallchief, ballet star who was inspiration for Balanchine, dies at 88." *Washington Post*, April 12, 2013. https://www.washingtonpost.com/local/obituaries/maria-tallchief-ballet-star-who-was-inspiration-for-balanchine-dies-at-88/2013/04/12/5888f3de-c5dc-11df-94e1-c5afa35a9e59_story.html?utm_term=.b7a15c638829.

Hansberry, Lorraine. *To Be Young, Gifted and Black*. Adapted by Robert Nemiroff. New York: Samuel French, Inc., 1971.

Hardorff, Richard G., ed. *Cheyenne Memories of the Custer Fight*. Lincoln: University of Nebraska Press, 1998.

History. "Hatshepsut." http://www.history.com/topics/ancient-history/hatshepsut.

History, "This Day in History, Fannie Farmer Opens Cooking School." http://www.history.com/this-day-in-history/fannie-farmer-opens-cooking-school.

Horwitz, Tony. "The Woman Who (Maybe) Struck out Babe Ruth and Lou Gehrig," *Smithsonian Magazine*, July 2013. https://www.smithsonianmag.com/history/the-woman-who-maybe-struck-out-babe-ruth-and-lou-gehrig-4759182/.

Hrala, Josh. "The Story of Japan's Deadly All-Female Ninja Squad." *Modern Notion*, March 17, 2015. http://modernnotion.com/the-story-of-japans-deadly-all-female-ninja-squad/.

IMDB. "Angela Morley." http://www.imdb.com/name/nm0605859/.

Inglis-Arkell, Esther. "We Had a Cure for Leprosy for Centuries, But Couldn't Get It to Work." *iO9*, May 8, 2015. http://io9.gizmodo.com/we-had-a-cure-for-leprosy-for-centuries-but-we-couldnt-1703005163.

Isabella Stewart Gardner Museum. http://www.gardnermuseum.org/home/.

James, Edward T., Janet Wilson James, and Paul S. Boyer. *Notable American Women, 1607-1950: A Biographical Dictionary, Volume 3*. Cambridge: Belknap Press, 1971.

Jones, Jonathan. "Top Hats off to Marie Duval, a lost Victorian cartoonist sensation." *Guardian*, October 27, 2014. https://www.theguardian.com/artanddesign/jonathanjonesblog/2014/oct/27/marie-duval-victorian-cartoonist-ally-sloper.

Juliette Gordon Low birthplace. http://www.juliettegordonlowbirthplace.org/.

"Kapampangan Rebels, Radicals and Renegades Who Changed Philippine History." *Singsing Magazine* 6, no. 1 (1998).

Katinka Hesselink. "'Kalakshetra' and Rukmini Devi." http://www.katinkahesselink.net/his/kalakshetra.html.

Kay, Karyn, and Gerald Peary. "Interview with Dorothy Arzner," *Agnès Films*, July 16, 2011. http://agnesfilms.com/interviews/interview-with-dorothy-arzner/.

Kelly Gardiner. "The Real Life of Julie d'Aubigny." https://kellygardiner.com/fiction/books/goddess/the-real-life-of-julie-daubigny/.

Khan, Sumara. "Fatima Al-Fihri: Founder of World's Very First University." *Why Islam?*, August 7, 2014. https://www.whyislam.org/muslim-heritage/fatima-al-fihri-founder-of-worlds-very-first-university/.

Kimball, Christopher. *Fannie's Last Supper*. New York: Hachette, 2010.

Kleiber, Shannon Henry. "Juliette Gordon Low, Who Had No Children of Her Own, Started Girl Scouts in 1912." *Washington Post*, March 9, 2012. https://www.washingtonpost.com/lifestyle/kidpost/juliette-gordon-low-who-had-no-children-of-her-own-started-girl-scouts-in-1912/2012/02/28/gIQA5CBO1R_story.html?utm_term=.6ecca3a1c7bb.

Krismann, Carol. *Encyclopedia of American Women in Business*. Westport, Connecticut: Greenwood Press, 2005.

Kroll, Chana. "Irena Sendler: Rescuer of the Children of Warsaw," TheJewishWoman.org. http://www.chabad.org/theJewishWoman/article_cdo/aid/939081/jewish/Irena-Sendler.htm.

Kunzle, David. "Marie Duval: A Caricaturist Rediscovered." *Woman's Art Journal* 7, no. 1 (Spring–Summer 1986): 26–31.

Kunzle, David. "The First Ally Sloper: The Earliest Popular Cartoon Character as a Satire on the Victorian Work Ethic." *Oxford Art Journal* 8:1 (1985): 40–48. doi: https://doi.org/10.1093/oxartj/8.1.40.

Lanzona, Vina A. *Amazons of the Huk Rebellion: Gender, Sex, and Revolution in the Philippines*. Madison: University of Wisconsin Press, 2009.

Lenz, Lyz. "The Scandalous Legacy of Isabella Stewart Gardner, Collector of Art and Men." *Broadly*, December 3, 2015. https://broadly.vice.com/en_us/article/the-scandalous-legacy-of-isabella-stewart-gardner-collector-of-art-and-men.

Li, Jessica. "Emily Warren Roebling. The Engineer Behind the Brooklyn Bridge." *Scientista*, January 16, 2015. http://www.scientistafoundation.com/scientista-spotlights/emily-roebling-the-engineer-behind-the-brooklyn-bridge.

Life in a Jar: The Irena Sendler Project. book and website: http://www.irenasendler.org/.

Lopez, Leticia. "Badass Ladies of History: Fatima Al-Fihri," *Germ Magazine*, October 18, 2016. http://www.germmagazine.com/badass-ladies-in-history-fatima-al-fihri/.

Lorraine Hansberry Literary Trust. http://lhlt.org/.

Ludington's Ride. "Sybil's Story." http://ludingtonsride.com/history.htm.

Lyme Regis Museum. "Mary Anning." http://www.lymeregismuseum.co.uk/collection/mary-anning/.

Macintyre, Ben. *Double Cross*. London: Bloomsbury, 2012.

Macintyre, Ben, "The Good Time Girl Who Fooled the Nazis," *Times*, March 26, 2012. http://www.thetimes.co.uk/tto/life/article3362598.ece.

Madam C. J. Walker Beauty Culture. "The Legacy of Madam C. J. Walker." http://www.mcjwbeautyculture.com/about-madam-c-j-walker-beauty-culture/#.WLmp3WQrKRs.

Maggs, Sam. *Wonder Women: 25 Innovators, Inventors, and Trailblazers Who Changed History*. Philadelphia: Quirk Books, 2016.

Marcus, Leonard S. *Dear Genius: The Letters of Ursula Nordstrom*. New York: HarperCollins, 2000.

Matera, Marc, Misty L. Bastian, and Susan Kingsley Kent. *The Women's War of 1929: Gender and Violence in Colonial Nigeria*. New York: Palgrave Macmillan, 2012.

Mayne, Judith. *Directed by Dorothy Arzner*. Bloomington: University of Indiana Press, 1994.

Mba, Nina Emma. *Nigerian Women Mobilized: Women's Political Activity in Southern Nigeria, 1900–1965*. Berkeley: Institute of International Studies, 1982.

McCullough, David. *The Great Bridge: The Epic Story of the Building of the Brooklyn Bridge*. New York: Simon and Schuster, 2011.

McDonnell, Patrick J. "Argentines Remember a Mother Who Joined the 'Disappeared.'" *Los Angeles Times*, March 24, 2006. http://articles.latimes.com/2006/mar/24/world/fg-dirtywar24.

Mendoza, Sylvia. *The Book of Latina Women*. Avon, Massachusetts: Adams Media, 2004.

Mernissi, Fatima. *The Forgotten Queens of Islam*. Translated by Mary Jo Lakeland. Minneapolis: University of Minnesota Press, 1993.

Moore, Jack. "The Woman Who Struck Out Babe Ruth and Lou Gehrig." *Vice Sports*, August 29, 2015. https://sports.vice.com/en_us/article/the-woman-who-struck-out-babe-ruth-and-lou-gehrig.

Morrow, James. "Emmy Noether," in *Notable Women in Mathematics: A Biographical Dictionary*, edited by Charlene Morrow and Teri Perl. Westport, Connecticut: Greenwood Press, 1998.

Mosher, Clelia Duel. *The Mosher Survey: Sexual Attitudes of 45 Victorian Women*. Arno Press, 1980.

Murray, Dian H. *Pirates of the South China Coast, 1790–1810*. Stanford: Stanford University Press, 1987.

National Army Museum. "Rani of Jhansi." http://www.nam.ac.uk/exhibitions/online-exhibitions/enemy-commanders-britains-greatest-foes/rani-jhansi.

National Geographic Education Staff. "Mary Seacole: Adventurer in Jamaica, Panama, and the Crimean War." *National Geographic*, November 27, 2013. http://www.nationalgeographic.org/news/mary-seacole/.

National Women's History Museum. "Historical Women Who Rocked: Jackie Mitchell." https://www.nwhm.org/articles/jackie-mitchell-and-bloomer-girls.

National Women's History Museum. "Sybil Ludington (1761–1839)." https://www.nwhm.org/education-resources/biography/biographies/sibyl-ludington/.

New World Encyclopedia. "Tru'ng Sisters." http://www.newworldencyclopedia.org/entry/Tr%C6%B0ng_Sisters.

Nigel Perrin. "SOE Agent Profiles: Noor Inayat Khan." http://nigelperrin.com/soe-noor-inayat-khan.htm#.Wl YmBPyuRo.

Noor Inayat Khan Memorial Trust. "Noor Inayat Khan." http://www.noormemorial.org/noor.php.

Oakes, Elizabeth H. *International Encyclopedia of Women Scientists*. Facts on File, 2002.

Orejas, Tonnette. "Liwayway, The Warrior Who Wore Lipstick in Gun Battles. Inquirer.net, May 17, 2014. http://newsinfo.inquirer.net/602758/liwayway-warrior-who-wore-lipstick-in-gun-battles.

Park, Thomas K., and Aomar Boum. *Historical Dictionary of Morocco*. Lanham, Maryland: Scarecrow Press, Inc., 2005.

PBS. "Irena Sendler: In the Name of Their Mothers." http://www.pbs.org/program/irena-sendler/.

Pierce, Patricia. *Jurassic Mary: Mary Anning and the Primeval Monsters*. Mount Pleasant, South Carolina: History Press, 2006.

Platoni, Kara. "The Sex Scholar." *Stanford Alumni*, March/April 2010. https://alumni.stanford.edu/get/page/magazine/article/?article_id=29954.

Plumer, Brad. "Emmy Noether Revolutionized Mathematics — and Still Faced Sexism all Her Life." *Vox*, March 23, 2016. http://www.vox.com/2015/3/23/8274777/emmy-noether.

Popova, Maria. "How Ursula Nordstrom, the Greatest Patron Saint of Modern Childhood Stood, Up for Creativity Against Commercial Cowardice." *Brain Pickings*. https://www.brainpickings.org/2015/02/02/ursula-nordstrom-letters-integrity/.

Project Vox. "Cavendish (1623–1673)." http://projectvox.library.duke.edu/content/cavendish-1623-1673.

Roberts, Jennifer Sherman. "Everyone, We Need to Talk About 17th-Century Badass Writer Margaret Cavendish." *The Mary Sue*, May 12, 2015. http://www.themarysue.com/margaret-cavendish/.

Robinson, Jane. *Mary Seacole: The Black Woman Who Invented Modern Nursing*. New York: Carroll & Graf Publishers, 2004.

Romano, Aja. "This 17th-Century Sword-Swinging Opera Singer Will Rule the Internet in 2013." *Daily Dot*, May 8, 2013. Last modified February 25, 2017. http://www.dailydot.com/culture/julie-daubigny-swordswoman-opera-singer-meme/.

Rossen, Jake. "The Female Jiu-Jitsu Crew That Defended Women's Rights." *Mental Floss*, 2015. http://mentalfloss.com/article/64502/female-jiu-jitsu-crew-defended-feminists-1900s-london.

Royall, Tyler. "Murasaki Shikibu." *Harvard Magazine*, May–June 2002. http://harvardmagazine.com/2002/05/murasaki-shikibu.html.

Ruz, Camila, and Justin Parkinson. "'Suffrajitsu': How the Suffragettes Fought Back Using Martial Arts." *BBC News*, October 5, 2015. http://www.bbc.com/news/magazine-34425615.

Saber, Latifa. "Did You Know That the First University Was Founded by a Muslim Woman?" *MVSLIM*. http://mvslim.com/inspiring-muslim-women-fatima-al-fihr/.

Sadie, Stanley (ed.). *The New Grove Dictionary of Opera*. Oxford, United Kingdom: Oxford University Press, 1992.

Salmonson, Jessica Amanda. *The Encyclopedia of Amazons: Women Warriors from Antiquity to the Modern Era*. New York: Anchor Books, 1991.

Sarasohn, Lisa T. *The Natural Philosophy of Margaret Cavendish: Reason and Fancy During the Scientific Revolution*. Baltimore: JHU Press, 2010.

ScholarSpace. Ball, Alice Augusta. https://scholarspace.manoa.hawaii.edu/handle/10125/1837.

Schwartz, John. "A Concealed Voice Rings Loud and Clear." *New York Times*, October 25, 2013. http://www.nytimes.com/2013/10/27/arts/artsspecial/a-concealed-voice-rings-loud-and-clear.html.

Seacole, Mary. *Wonderful Adventures of Mrs. Seacole in Many Lands*. London: James Blackwood Paternoster Row, 1857.

Silver, Carly. "These Ancient Vietnamese Sisters Rebelled Against the Chinese with a Co-Ed Army." *History Buff*, January 19, 2016. http://historybuff.com/these-ancient-vietnamese-sisters-led-rebellion-against-chinese-YP62DM95DgyJ.

Sinkler, Rebecca Pepper. "Confessions of a Former Child." *New York Times*, March 22, 1998. http://www.nytimes.com/books/98/03/22/reviews/980322.22sinklet.html.

Smith, William, ed. "Agno'dice." *A Dictionary of Greek and Roman Biography and Myth*. http://www.perseus.tufts.edu/hopper/text?doc=Perseus%3Atext%3A1999.04.0104%3Aentry%3Dagnodice-bio-1.

Strange Science. "Mary Anning." http://www.strangescience.net/anning.htm.

Tallchief, Maria, and Larry Kaplan. *Maria Tallchief: America's Prima Ballerina*. New York: Henry Holt, 1997.

Teaching Tolerance: A Project of the Southern Poverty Law Center. "Madres de Plaza de Mayo." http://www.tolerance.org/activity/madres-de-plaza-de-mayo.

The Marie Duval Archive. http://www.marieduval.org/.

The San Diego Supercomputer Presents Women in Science: A Selection of 16 Significant Contributors. "Annie Jump Cannon." https://www.sdsc.edu/ScienceWomen/cannon.html.

"The Tale of Murasaki Shikibu." *Economist*, December 23, 1999. http://www.economist.com/node/347504.

The Theosophical Society in America. https://www.theosophical.org/.

The Trung Sisters vs China. Stuff You Missed in History Class. Podcast audio, August 30, 2010. http://www.missedinhistory.com/podcasts/the-trung-sisters-vs-china.htm.

University of California Museum of Palaeontology. "Mary Anning (1799–1847)." http://www.ucmp.berkeley.edu/history/anning.html.

Qweenzone. "The Tale of Queen Arawelo: The Original Feminist." Last modified October 23, 2015. https://qweenzone.wordpress.com/2015/10/23/the-tale-of-queen-arawelo-the-original-feminist/.

University of Virginia. "Women in Medicine: Agnodice and Childbirth." http://exhibits.hsl.virginia.edu/antiqua/women/.

Wagner, Tricia Martineau. *African American Women of the Old West*. Guilford, Connecticut: TwoDot Books, 2007.

Weatherford, Jack. "The Wrestler Princess." *Lapham's Quarterly*, September 27, 2010. http://laphamsquarterly.org/roundtable/wrestler-princess.

Wellesley College. "Annie Jump Cannon (1863–1941)." Last modified July 26, 2006. http://academics.wellesley.edu/Astronomy/Annie/.

Wells, Diana. *Lives of the Trees: An Uncommon History*. Chapel Hill: Algonquin Books, 2010.

Whitbread, Helena, ed. *I Know My Own Heart: The Diaries of Anne Lister*. New York: New York University Press, 1988.

Wieringa, Saskia, ed. *Subversive Women: Historical Experiences of Gender and Resistance*. London: Zed Books, 1997.

Williams, Rachel. "Edith Garrud: A Public Vote for the Suffragette who Taught Martial Arts." *Guardian*, June 25, 2012. https://www.theguardian.com/lifeandstyle/2012/jun/25/edith-garrud-suffragette-martial-arts.

Wilson, Elizabeth B. "The Queen Who Would be King." *Smithsonian Magazine*, September 2006. http://www.smithsonianmag.com/history/the-queen-who-would-be-king-130328511/.

Wise, Damon. "Lumière Festival: Dorothy Arzner, a Hollywood Trailblazer." *Variety*, October 10, 2016. http://variety.com/2016/film/festivals/dorothy-arzner-lumiere-festival-hollywood-golden-age-director-1201883604/.

Wishart, David J., ed. *Encyclopedia of the Great Plains*. Lincoln: University of Nebraska Press, 2004.

Women Film Pioneers Project. "Dorothy Arzner." https://wfpp.cdrs.columbia.edu/pioneer/ccp-dorothy-arzner/.

Women You Should Know. "Thanks to a Bug Landing in Her Imperial Tea (c. 2640 BC), We Have Silk." Last modified March 25, 2014. http://www.womenyoushouldknow.net/thanks-bug-landing-imperial-tea-silk/.

Woodman, Jenny. "The Women Astronomers Who Revolutionized Astronomy." *Atlantic*, December 2, 2016. https://www.theatlantic.com/science/archive/2016/12/the-women-computers-who-measured-the-stars/509231/.

Young, Lauren. "Marie Duval, the Pioneering 19th-Century Cartoonist That History Forgot." *Atlas Obscura*, February 1, 2017. http://www.atlasobscura.com/articles/marie-duval-the-pioneering-19th-century-cartoonist-that-history-forgot.

Yule, Henry (ed.). *The Book of Ser Marco Polo, the Venetian*. Originally printed London: J. Murray, 1871.

Zielinski, Sarah. "Mary Anning, an Amazing Fossil Hunter." *Smithsonian.com*, January 5, 2010. http://www.smithsonianmag.com/science-nature/mary-anning-an-amazing-fossil-hunter-60691902/.